C-3205   CAREER EXAMINATION SERIES

This is your
PASSBOOK for...

Nursing Home Administrator

Test Preparation Study Guide
Questions & Answers

COPYRIGHT NOTICE

This book is SOLELY intended for, is sold ONLY to, and its use is RESTRICTED to individual, bona fide applicants or candidates who qualify by virtue of having seriously filed applications for appropriate license, certificate, professional and/or promotional advancement, higher school matriculation, scholarship, or other legitimate requirements of education and/or governmental authorities.

This book is NOT intended for use, class instruction, tutoring, training, duplication, copying, reprinting, excerption, or adaptation, etc., by:

1) Other publishers
2) Proprietors and/or Instructors of "Coaching" and/or Preparatory Courses
3) Personnel and/or Training Divisions of commercial, industrial, and governmental organizations
4) Schools, colleges, or universities and/or their departments and staffs, including teachers and other personnel
5) Testing Agencies or Bureaus
6) Study groups which seek by the purchase of a single volume to copy and/or duplicate and/or adapt this material for use by the group as a whole without having purchased individual volumes for each of the members of the group
7) Et al.

Such persons would be in violation of appropriate Federal and State statutes.

PROVISION OF LICENSING AGREEMENTS – Recognized educational, commercial, industrial, and governmental institutions and organizations, and others legitimately engaged in educational pursuits, including training, testing, and measurement activities, may address request for a licensing agreement to the copyright owners, who will determine whether, and under what conditions, including fees and charges, the materials in this book may be used them. In other words, a licensing facility exists for the legitimate use of the material in this book on other than an individual basis. However, it is asseverated and affirmed here that the material in this book CANNOT be used without the receipt of the express permission of such a licensing agreement from the Publishers. Inquiries re licensing should be addressed to the company, attention rights and permissions department.

All rights reserved, including the right of reproduction in whole or in part, in any form or by any means, electronic or mechanical, including photocopying, recording, or by any information storage and retrieval system, without permission in writing from the Publisher.

Copyright © 2024 by
National Learning Corporation

212 Michael Drive, Syosset, NY 11791
(516) 921-8888 • www.passbooks.com
E-mail: info@passbooks.com

PASSBOOK® SERIES

THE *PASSBOOK® SERIES* has been created to prepare applicants and candidates for the ultimate academic battlefield – the examination room.

At some time in our lives, each and every one of us may be required to take an examination – for validation, matriculation, admission, qualification, registration, certification, or licensure.

Based on the assumption that every applicant or candidate has met the basic formal educational standards, has taken the required number of courses, and read the necessary texts, the *PASSBOOK® SERIES* furnishes the one special preparation which may assure passing with confidence, instead of failing with insecurity. Examination questions – together with answers – are furnished as the basic vehicle for study so that the mysteries of the examination and its compounding difficulties may be eliminated or diminished by a sure method.

This book is meant to help you pass your examination provided that you qualify and are serious in your objective.

The entire field is reviewed through the huge store of content information which is succinctly presented through a provocative and challenging approach – the question-and-answer method.

A climate of success is established by furnishing the correct answers at the end of each test.

You soon learn to recognize types of questions, forms of questions, and patterns of questioning. You may even begin to anticipate expected outcomes.

You perceive that many questions are repeated or adapted so that you can gain acute insights, which may enable you to score many sure points.

You learn how to confront new questions, or types of questions, and to attack them confidently and work out the correct answers.

You note objectives and emphases, and recognize pitfalls and dangers, so that you may make positive educational adjustments.

Moreover, you are kept fully informed in relation to new concepts, methods, practices, and directions in the field.

You discover that you are actually taking the examination all the time: you are preparing for the examination by "taking" an examination, not by reading extraneous and/or supererogatory textbooks.

In short, this PASSBOOK®, used directedly, should be an important factor in helping you to pass your test.

NURSING HOME ADMINISTRATOR

DUTIES

Administers, directs and coordinates all activities of the facility to carry out its objectives as to the care of sick, injured, convalescent, aged or infirm patients, the furtherance of scientific knowledge and the promotion of community health; carries out programs within policies and by general directive from a governing board or owners; promotes favorable public relations; negotiates for improvement of building and equipment; coordinates activities of medical and professional staffs with those of other departments; recommends and develops policies and procedures for various facility activities; performs related administrative and supervisory duties to insure efficient operation of the facility; bears the responsibility for efficient functioning and coordination of all departments, program planning, organization of departments, control of activities, budgeting, interpreting and administering policies of the governing body or owners and insures that patients receive the highest level of professional and medical care.

SCOPE OF THE EXAMINATION

1. Applicable standards of environmental health and safety
    a. Hygiene and sanitation
    b. Communicable diseases
    c. Management of isolation
    d. The total environment
    e. Elements of accident prevention
    f. Special architectural needs of nursing home patients
    g. Drug handling and control
    h. Safety factors in oxygen usage

2. Local health and safety regulations – Guidelines vary according to local provisions

3. General administration
    a. Institutional administration
    b. Planning, organizing, directing, controlling, staffing, coordinating and budgeting
    c. Human relations
        i. Management/employee interrelationships
        ii. Management/family interrelationships
        iii. Employee/employee interrelationships
        iv. Employee/patient interrelationships
        v. Employee/family interrelationships
    d. Training of personnel
        i. Training of employees to become sensitive to patient needs
        ii. Ongoing in-service training/education

4. Psychology of patient care
   a. Anxiety
   b. Depression
   c. Drugs, alcohol and their effect
   d. Motivation
   e. Separation reaction

5. Principles of medical care
   a. Anatomy and physiology
   b. Psychology
   c. Disease recognition
   d. Disease process
   e. Nutrition
   f. Aging processes
   g. Medical terminology
   h. Materia Medica
   i. Medical Social Service
   j. Utilization review
   k. Professional and medical ethics

6. Personal and social care
   a. Resident and patient care planning
   b. Activity programming:
      i. Patient participation
      ii. Recreation
   c. Environmental adjustment. Interrelationships between patient and:
      i. Patient
      ii. Staff
      iii. Family and friends
      iv. Administrator
      v. Management
   d. Rehabilitation and restorative activities:
      i. Training in activities of daily living
      ii. Techniques of group therapy
   e. Interdisciplinary interpretation of patient care to:
      i. The patient
      ii. The staff
      iii. The family

7. Therapeutic and supportive care and services in long-term care
    a. Individual care planning as it embraces all therapeutic care and supportive services
    b. Meaningful observations of patient behavior as related to total patient care
    c. Interdisciplinary evaluation and revision of patient care plans and procedures
    d. Unique aspects and requirements of geriatric patient care
    e. Professional staff interrelationships with patient's physician
    f. Rehabilitative and remotivational role of individual therapeutic and supportive services
    g. Psychological, social and religious needs, in addition to physical need of patient
    h. Needs for dental service

8. Departmental organization and management
    a. Criteria for coordinating establishment of departmental and unit objectives
    b. Reporting and accountability of individual department to administrator
    c. Criteria for departmental evaluation
    d. Techniques of providing adequate professional therapeutic supportive and administrative services
    e. The following departments may be used in relating matters of organization and management:
        i. Nursing
        ii. Housekeeping
        iii. Dietary
        iv. Laundry
        v. Pharmaceutical services
        vi. Social service
        vii. Business office
        viii. Recreation
        ix. Medical records
        x. Admitting
        xi. Physical therapy
        xii. Occupational therapy
        xiii. Medical and dental services
        xiv. Laboratories
        xv. X-ray
        xvi. Maintenance

9. Community Interrelationships
    a. Community medical care, rehabilitative and social services resources
    b. Other community resources:
        i. Religious institutions
        ii. Schools
        iii. Service agencies
        iv. Government agencies
        v. Consumers
    c. Third party payment organizations
    d. Comprehensive health planning agencies
    e. Volunteers and auxiliaries

HOW TO TAKE A TEST

I. YOU MUST PASS AN EXAMINATION

A. WHAT EVERY CANDIDATE SHOULD KNOW

Examination applicants often ask us for help in preparing for the written test. What can I study in advance? What kinds of questions will be asked? How will the test be given? How will the papers be graded?

As an applicant for a civil service examination, you may be wondering about some of these things. Our purpose here is to suggest effective methods of advance study and to describe civil service examinations.

Your chances for success on this examination can be increased if you know how to prepare. Those "pre-examination jitters" can be reduced if you know what to expect. You can even experience an adventure in good citizenship if you know why civil service exams are given.

B. WHY ARE CIVIL SERVICE EXAMINATIONS GIVEN?

Civil service examinations are important to you in two ways. As a citizen, you want public jobs filled by employees who know how to do their work. As a job seeker, you want a fair chance to compete for that job on an equal footing with other candidates. The best-known means of accomplishing this two-fold goal is the competitive examination.

Exams are widely publicized throughout the nation. They may be administered for jobs in federal, state, city, municipal, town or village governments or agencies.

Any citizen may apply, with some limitations, such as the age or residence of applicants. Your experience and education may be reviewed to see whether you meet the requirements for the particular examination. When these requirements exist, they are reasonable and applied consistently to all applicants. Thus, a competitive examination may cause you some uneasiness now, but it is your privilege and safeguard.

C. HOW ARE CIVIL SERVICE EXAMS DEVELOPED?

Examinations are carefully written by trained technicians who are specialists in the field known as "psychological measurement," in consultation with recognized authorities in the field of work that the test will cover. These experts recommend the subject matter areas or skills to be tested; only those knowledges or skills important to your success on the job are included. The most reliable books and source materials available are used as references. Together, the experts and technicians judge the difficulty level of the questions.

Test technicians know how to phrase questions so that the problem is clearly stated. Their ethics do not permit "trick" or "catch" questions. Questions may have been tried out on sample groups, or subjected to statistical analysis, to determine their usefulness.

Written tests are often used in combination with performance tests, ratings of training and experience, and oral interviews. All of these measures combine to form the best-known means of finding the right person for the right job.

II. HOW TO PASS THE WRITTEN TEST

A. NATURE OF THE EXAMINATION

To prepare intelligently for civil service examinations, you should know how they differ from school examinations you have taken. In school you were assigned certain definite pages to read or subjects to cover. The examination questions were quite detailed and usually emphasized memory. Civil service exams, on the other hand, try to discover your present ability to perform the duties of a position, plus your potentiality to learn these duties. In other words, a civil service exam attempts to predict how successful you will be. Questions cover such a broad area that they cannot be as minute and detailed as school exam questions.

In the public service similar kinds of work, or positions, are grouped together in one "class." This process is known as *position-classification*. All the positions in a class are paid according to the salary range for that class. One class title covers all of these positions, and they are all tested by the same examination.

B. FOUR BASIC STEPS

1) Study the announcement

How, then, can you know what subjects to study? Our best answer is: "Learn as much as possible about the class of positions for which you've applied." The exam will test the knowledge, skills and abilities needed to do the work.

Your most valuable source of information about the position you want is the official exam announcement. This announcement lists the training and experience qualifications. Check these standards and apply only if you come reasonably close to meeting them.

The brief description of the position in the examination announcement offers some clues to the subjects which will be tested. Think about the job itself. Review the duties in your mind. Can you perform them, or are there some in which you are rusty? Fill in the blank spots in your preparation.

Many jurisdictions preview the written test in the exam announcement by including a section called "Knowledge and Abilities Required," "Scope of the Examination," or some similar heading. Here you will find out specifically what fields will be tested.

2) Review your own background

Once you learn in general what the position is all about, and what you need to know to do the work, ask yourself which subjects you already know fairly well and which need improvement. You may wonder whether to concentrate on improving your strong areas or on building some background in your fields of weakness. When the announcement has specified "some knowledge" or "considerable knowledge," or has used adjectives like "beginning principles of..." or "advanced ... methods," you can get a clue as to the number and difficulty of questions to be asked in any given field. More questions, and hence broader coverage, would be included for those subjects which are more important in the work. Now weigh your strengths and weaknesses against the job requirements and prepare accordingly.

3) Determine the level of the position

Another way to tell how intensively you should prepare is to understand the level of the job for which you are applying. Is it the entering level? In other words, is this the position in which beginners in a field of work are hired? Or is it an intermediate or advanced level? Sometimes this is indicated by such words as "Junior" or "Senior" in the class title. Other jurisdictions use Roman numerals to designate the level – Clerk I, Clerk II, for example. The word "Supervisor" sometimes appears in the title. If the level is not indicated by the title, check the description of duties. Will you be working under very close supervision, or will you have responsibility for independent decisions in this work?

4) Choose appropriate study materials

Now that you know the subjects to be examined and the relative amount of each subject to be covered, you can choose suitable study materials. For beginning level jobs, or even advanced ones, if you have a pronounced weakness in some aspect of your training, read a modern, standard textbook in that field. Be sure it is up to date and has general coverage. Such books are normally available at your library, and the librarian will be glad to help you locate one. For entry-level positions, questions of appropriate difficulty are chosen – neither highly advanced questions, nor those too simple. Such questions require careful thought but not advanced training.

If the position for which you are applying is technical or advanced, you will read more advanced, specialized material. If you are already familiar with the basic principles of your field, elementary textbooks would waste your time. Concentrate on advanced textbooks and technical periodicals. Think through the concepts and review difficult problems in your field.

These are all general sources. You can get more ideas on your own initiative, following these leads. For example, training manuals and publications of the government agency which employs workers in your field can be useful, particularly for technical and professional positions. A letter or visit to the government department involved may result in more specific study suggestions, and certainly will provide you with a more definite idea of the exact nature of the position you are seeking.

III. KINDS OF TESTS

Tests are used for purposes other than measuring knowledge and ability to perform specified duties. For some positions, it is equally important to test ability to make adjustments to new situations or to profit from training. In others, basic mental abilities not dependent on information are essential. Questions which test these things may not appear as pertinent to the duties of the position as those which test for knowledge and information. Yet they are often highly important parts of a fair examination. For very general questions, it is almost impossible to help you direct your study efforts. What we can do is to point out some of the more common of these general abilities needed in public service positions and describe some typical questions.

1) General information

Broad, general information has been found useful for predicting job success in some kinds of work. This is tested in a variety of ways, from vocabulary lists to questions about current events. Basic background in some field of work, such as sociology or economics, may be sampled in a group of questions. Often these are principles which have become familiar to most persons through exposure rather than through formal training. It is difficult to advise you how to study for these questions; being alert to the world around you is our best suggestion.

2) Verbal ability

An example of an ability needed in many positions is verbal or language ability. Verbal ability is, in brief, the ability to use and understand words. Vocabulary and grammar tests are typical measures of this ability. Reading comprehension or paragraph interpretation questions are common in many kinds of civil service tests. You are given a paragraph of written material and asked to find its central meaning.

3) **Numerical ability**

Number skills can be tested by the familiar arithmetic problem, by checking paired lists of numbers to see which are alike and which are different, or by interpreting charts and graphs. In the latter test, a graph may be printed in the test booklet which you are asked to use as the basis for answering questions.

4) **Observation**

A popular test for law-enforcement positions is the observation test. A picture is shown to you for several minutes, then taken away. Questions about the picture test your ability to observe both details and larger elements.

5) **Following directions**

In many positions in the public service, the employee must be able to carry out written instructions dependably and accurately. You may be given a chart with several columns, each column listing a variety of information. The questions require you to carry out directions involving the information given in the chart.

6) **Skills and aptitudes**

Performance tests effectively measure some manual skills and aptitudes. When the skill is one in which you are trained, such as typing or shorthand, you can practice. These tests are often very much like those given in business school or high school courses. For many of the other skills and aptitudes, however, no short-time preparation can be made. Skills and abilities natural to you or that you have developed throughout your lifetime are being tested.

Many of the general questions just described provide all the data needed to answer the questions and ask you to use your reasoning ability to find the answers. Your best preparation for these tests, as well as for tests of facts and ideas, is to be at your physical and mental best. You, no doubt, have your own methods of getting into an exam-taking mood and keeping "in shape." The next section lists some ideas on this subject.

IV. KINDS OF QUESTIONS

Only rarely is the "essay" question, which you answer in narrative form, used in civil service tests. Civil service tests are usually of the short-answer type. Full instructions for answering these questions will be given to you at the examination. But in case this is your first experience with short-answer questions and separate answer sheets, here is what you need to know:

1) Multiple-choice Questions

Most popular of the short-answer questions is the "multiple choice" or "best answer" question. It can be used, for example, to test for factual knowledge, ability to solve problems or judgment in meeting situations found at work.

A multiple-choice question is normally one of three types—
- It can begin with an incomplete statement followed by several possible endings. You are to find the one ending which *best* completes the statement, although some of the others may not be entirely wrong.
- It can also be a complete statement in the form of a question which is answered by choosing one of the statements listed.

- It can be in the form of a problem – again you select the best answer.

Here is an example of a multiple-choice question with a discussion which should give you some clues as to the method for choosing the right answer:

When an employee has a complaint about his assignment, the action which will *best* help him overcome his difficulty is to
      A. discuss his difficulty with his coworkers
      B. take the problem to the head of the organization
      C. take the problem to the person who gave him the assignment
      D. say nothing to anyone about his complaint

In answering this question, you should study each of the choices to find which is best. Consider choice "A" – Certainly an employee may discuss his complaint with fellow employees, but no change or improvement can result, and the complaint remains unresolved. Choice "B" is a poor choice since the head of the organization probably does not know what assignment you have been given, and taking your problem to him is known as "going over the head" of the supervisor. The supervisor, or person who made the assignment, is the person who can clarify it or correct any injustice. Choice "C" is, therefore, correct. To say nothing, as in choice "D," is unwise. Supervisors have and interest in knowing the problems employees are facing, and the employee is seeking a solution to his problem.

2) True/False Questions

The "true/false" or "right/wrong" form of question is sometimes used. Here a complete statement is given. Your job is to decide whether the statement is right or wrong.

SAMPLE: A roaming cell-phone call to a nearby city costs less than a non-roaming call to a distant city.

This statement is wrong, or false, since roaming calls are more expensive.

This is not a complete list of all possible question forms, although most of the others are variations of these common types. You will always get complete directions for answering questions. Be sure you understand *how* to mark your answers – ask questions until you do.

V. RECORDING YOUR ANSWERS

Computer terminals are used more and more today for many different kinds of exams.
For an examination with very few applicants, you may be told to record your answers in the test booklet itself. Separate answer sheets are much more common. If this separate answer sheet is to be scored by machine – and this is often the case – it is highly important that you mark your answers correctly in order to get credit.
An electronic scoring machine is often used in civil service offices because of the speed with which papers can be scored. Machine-scored answer sheets must be marked with a pencil, which will be given to you. This pencil has a high graphite content which responds to the electronic scoring machine. As a matter of fact, stray dots may register as answers, so do not let your pencil rest on the answer sheet while you are pondering the correct answer. Also, if your pencil lead breaks or is otherwise defective, ask for another.

Since the answer sheet will be dropped in a slot in the scoring machine, be careful not to bend the corners or get the paper crumpled.

The answer sheet normally has five vertical columns of numbers, with 30 numbers to a column. These numbers correspond to the question numbers in your test booklet. After each number, going across the page are four or five pairs of dotted lines. These short dotted lines have small letters or numbers above them. The first two pairs may also have a "T" or "F" above the letters. This indicates that the first two pairs only are to be used if the questions are of the true-false type. If the questions are multiple choice, disregard the "T" and "F" and pay attention only to the small letters or numbers.

Answer your questions in the manner of the sample that follows:

32. The largest city in the United States is
    A. Washington, D.C.
    B. New York City
    C. Chicago
    D. Detroit
    E. San Francisco

1) Choose the answer you think is best. (New York City is the largest, so "B" is correct.)
2) Find the row of dotted lines numbered the same as the question you are answering. (Find row number 32)
3) Find the pair of dotted lines corresponding to the answer. (Find the pair of lines under the mark "B.")
4) Make a solid black mark between the dotted lines.

VI. BEFORE THE TEST

Common sense will help you find procedures to follow to get ready for an examination. Too many of us, however, overlook these sensible measures. Indeed, nervousness and fatigue have been found to be the most serious reasons why applicants fail to do their best on civil service tests. Here is a list of reminders:

- Begin your preparation early – Don't wait until the last minute to go scurrying around for books and materials or to find out what the position is all about.
- Prepare continuously – An hour a night for a week is better than an all-night cram session. This has been definitely established. What is more, a night a week for a month will return better dividends than crowding your study into a shorter period of time.
- Locate the place of the exam – You have been sent a notice telling you when and where to report for the examination. If the location is in a different town or otherwise unfamiliar to you, it would be well to inquire the best route and learn something about the building.
- Relax the night before the test – Allow your mind to rest. Do not study at all that night. Plan some mild recreation or diversion; then go to bed early and get a good night's sleep.
- Get up early enough to make a leisurely trip to the place for the test – This way unforeseen events, traffic snarls, unfamiliar buildings, etc. will not upset you.
- Dress comfortably – A written test is not a fashion show. You will be known by number and not by name, so wear something comfortable.

- Leave excess paraphernalia at home – Shopping bags and odd bundles will get in your way. You need bring only the items mentioned in the official notice you received; usually everything you need is provided. Do not bring reference books to the exam. They will only confuse those last minutes and be taken away from you when in the test room.
- Arrive somewhat ahead of time – If because of transportation schedules you must get there very early, bring a newspaper or magazine to take your mind off yourself while waiting.
- Locate the examination room – When you have found the proper room, you will be directed to the seat or part of the room where you will sit. Sometimes you are given a sheet of instructions to read while you are waiting. Do not fill out any forms until you are told to do so; just read them and be prepared.
- Relax and prepare to listen to the instructions
- If you have any physical problem that may keep you from doing your best, be sure to tell the test administrator. If you are sick or in poor health, you really cannot do your best on the exam. You can come back and take the test some other time.

VII. AT THE TEST

The day of the test is here and you have the test booklet in your hand. The temptation to get going is very strong. Caution! There is more to success than knowing the right answers. You must know how to identify your papers and understand variations in the type of short-answer question used in this particular examination. Follow these suggestions for maximum results from your efforts:

1) Cooperate with the monitor
The test administrator has a duty to create a situation in which you can be as much at ease as possible. He will give instructions, tell you when to begin, check to see that you are marking your answer sheet correctly, and so on. He is not there to guard you, although he will see that your competitors do not take unfair advantage. He wants to help you do your best.

2) Listen to all instructions
Don't jump the gun! Wait until you understand all directions. In most civil service tests you get more time than you need to answer the questions. So don't be in a hurry. Read each word of instructions until you clearly understand the meaning. Study the examples, listen to all announcements and follow directions. Ask questions if you do not understand what to do.

3) Identify your papers
Civil service exams are usually identified by number only. You will be assigned a number; you must not put your name on your test papers. Be sure to copy your number correctly. Since more than one exam may be given, copy your exact examination title.

4) Plan your time
Unless you are told that a test is a "speed" or "rate of work" test, speed itself is usually not important. Time enough to answer all the questions will be provided, but this does not mean that you have all day. An overall time limit has been set. Divide the total time (in minutes) by the number of questions to determine the approximate time you have for each question.

5) Do not linger over difficult questions

If you come across a difficult question, mark it with a paper clip (useful to have along) and come back to it when you have been through the booklet. One caution if you do this – be sure to skip a number on your answer sheet as well. Check often to be sure that you have not lost your place and that you are marking in the row numbered the same as the question you are answering.

6) Read the questions

Be sure you know what the question asks! Many capable people are unsuccessful because they failed to *read* the questions correctly.

7) Answer all questions

Unless you have been instructed that a penalty will be deducted for incorrect answers, it is better to guess than to omit a question.

8) Speed tests

It is often better NOT to guess on speed tests. It has been found that on timed tests people are tempted to spend the last few seconds before time is called in marking answers at random – without even reading them – in the hope of picking up a few extra points. To discourage this practice, the instructions may warn you that your score will be "corrected" for guessing. That is, a penalty will be applied. The incorrect answers will be deducted from the correct ones, or some other penalty formula will be used.

9) Review your answers

If you finish before time is called, go back to the questions you guessed or omitted to give them further thought. Review other answers if you have time.

10) Return your test materials

If you are ready to leave before others have finished or time is called, take ALL your materials to the monitor and leave quietly. Never take any test material with you. The monitor can discover whose papers are not complete, and taking a test booklet may be grounds for disqualification.

VIII. EXAMINATION TECHNIQUES

1) Read the general instructions carefully. These are usually printed on the first page of the exam booklet. As a rule, these instructions refer to the timing of the examination; the fact that you should not start work until the signal and must stop work at a signal, etc. If there are any *special* instructions, such as a choice of questions to be answered, make sure that you note this instruction carefully.

2) When you are ready to start work on the examination, that is as soon as the signal has been given, read the instructions to each question booklet, underline any key words or phrases, such as *least*, *best*, *outline*, *describe* and the like. In this way you will tend to answer as requested rather than discover on reviewing your paper that you *listed without describing*, that you selected the *worst* choice rather than the *best* choice, etc.

3) If the examination is of the objective or multiple-choice type – that is, each question will also give a series of possible answers: A, B, C or D, and you are called upon to select the best answer and write the letter next to that answer on your answer paper – it is advisable to start answering each question in turn. There may be anywhere from 50 to 100 such questions in the three or four hours allotted and you can see how much time would be taken if you read through all the questions before beginning to answer any. Furthermore, if you come across a question or group of questions which you know would be difficult to answer, it would undoubtedly affect your handling of all the other questions.

4) If the examination is of the essay type and contains but a few questions, it is a moot point as to whether you should read all the questions before starting to answer any one. Of course, if you are given a choice – say five out of seven and the like – then it is essential to read all the questions so you can eliminate the two that are most difficult. If, however, you are asked to answer all the questions, there may be danger in trying to answer the easiest one first because you may find that you will spend too much time on it. The best technique is to answer the first question, then proceed to the second, etc.

5) Time your answers. Before the exam begins, write down the time it started, then add the time allowed for the examination and write down the time it must be completed, then divide the time available somewhat as follows:
   - If 3-1/2 hours are allowed, that would be 210 minutes. If you have 80 objective-type questions, that would be an average of 2-1/2 minutes per question. Allow yourself no more than 2 minutes per question, or a total of 160 minutes, which will permit about 50 minutes to review.
   - If for the time allotment of 210 minutes there are 7 essay questions to answer, that would average about 30 minutes a question. Give yourself only 25 minutes per question so that you have about 35 minutes to review.

6) The most important instruction is to *read each question* and make sure you know what is wanted. The second most important instruction is to *time yourself properly* so that you answer every question. The third most important instruction is to *answer every question*. Guess if you have to but include something for each question. Remember that you will receive no credit for a blank and will probably receive some credit if you write something in answer to an essay question. If you guess a letter – say "B" for a multiple-choice question – you may have guessed right. If you leave a blank as an answer to a multiple-choice question, the examiners may respect your feelings but it will not add a point to your score. Some exams may penalize you for wrong answers, so in such cases *only*, you may not want to guess unless you have some basis for your answer.

7) Suggestions
   a. Objective-type questions
      1. Examine the question booklet for proper sequence of pages and questions
      2. Read all instructions carefully
      3. Skip any question which seems too difficult; return to it after all other questions have been answered
      4. Apportion your time properly; do not spend too much time on any single question or group of questions

5. Note and underline key words – *all, most, fewest, least, best, worst, same, opposite*, etc.
6. Pay particular attention to negatives
7. Note unusual option, e.g., unduly long, short, complex, different or similar in content to the body of the question
8. Observe the use of "hedging" words – *probably, may, most likely*, etc.
9. Make sure that your answer is put next to the same number as the question
10. Do not second-guess unless you have good reason to believe the second answer is definitely more correct
11. Cross out original answer if you decide another answer is more accurate; do not erase until you are ready to hand your paper in
12. Answer all questions; guess unless instructed otherwise
13. Leave time for review

b. Essay questions
   1. Read each question carefully
   2. Determine exactly what is wanted. Underline key words or phrases.
   3. Decide on outline or paragraph answer
   4. Include many different points and elements unless asked to develop any one or two points or elements
   5. Show impartiality by giving pros and cons unless directed to select one side only
   6. Make and write down any assumptions you find necessary to answer the questions
   7. Watch your English, grammar, punctuation and choice of words
   8. Time your answers; don't crowd material

8) Answering the essay question

Most essay questions can be answered by framing the specific response around several key words or ideas. Here are a few such key words or ideas:

M's: manpower, materials, methods, money, management
P's: purpose, program, policy, plan, procedure, practice, problems, pitfalls, personnel, public relations

   a. Six basic steps in handling problems:
      1. Preliminary plan and background development
      2. Collect information, data and facts
      3. Analyze and interpret information, data and facts
      4. Analyze and develop solutions as well as make recommendations
      5. Prepare report and sell recommendations
      6. Install recommendations and follow up effectiveness

   b. Pitfalls to avoid
      1. *Taking things for granted* – A statement of the situation does not necessarily imply that each of the elements is necessarily true; for example, a complaint may be invalid and biased so that all that can be taken for granted is that a complaint has been registered

2. *Considering only one side of a situation* – Wherever possible, indicate several alternatives and then point out the reasons you selected the best one
3. *Failing to indicate follow up* – Whenever your answer indicates action on your part, make certain that you will take proper follow-up action to see how successful your recommendations, procedures or actions turn out to be
4. *Taking too long in answering any single question* – Remember to time your answers properly

IX. AFTER THE TEST

Scoring procedures differ in detail among civil service jurisdictions although the general principles are the same. Whether the papers are hand-scored or graded by machine we have described, they are nearly always graded by number. That is, the person who marks the paper knows only the number – never the name – of the applicant. Not until all the papers have been graded will they be matched with names. If other tests, such as training and experience or oral interview ratings have been given, scores will be combined. Different parts of the examination usually have different weights. For example, the written test might count 60 percent of the final grade, and a rating of training and experience 40 percent. In many jurisdictions, veterans will have a certain number of points added to their grades.

After the final grade has been determined, the names are placed in grade order and an eligible list is established. There are various methods for resolving ties between those who get the same final grade – probably the most common is to place first the name of the person whose application was received first. Job offers are made from the eligible list in the order the names appear on it. You will be notified of your grade and your rank as soon as all these computations have been made. This will be done as rapidly as possible.

People who are found to meet the requirements in the announcement are called "eligibles." Their names are put on a list of eligible candidates. An eligible's chances of getting a job depend on how high he stands on this list and how fast agencies are filling jobs from the list.

When a job is to be filled from a list of eligibles, the agency asks for the names of people on the list of eligibles for that job. When the civil service commission receives this request, it sends to the agency the names of the three people highest on this list. Or, if the job to be filled has specialized requirements, the office sends the agency the names of the top three persons who meet these requirements from the general list.

The appointing officer makes a choice from among the three people whose names were sent to him. If the selected person accepts the appointment, the names of the others are put back on the list to be considered for future openings.

That is the rule in hiring from all kinds of eligible lists, whether they are for typist, carpenter, chemist, or something else. For every vacancy, the appointing officer has his choice of any one of the top three eligibles on the list. This explains why the person whose name is on top of the list sometimes does not get an appointment when some of the persons lower on the list do. If the appointing officer chooses the second or third eligible, the No. 1 eligible does not get a job at once, but stays on the list until he is appointed or the list is terminated.

X. HOW TO PASS THE INTERVIEW TEST

The examination for which you applied requires an oral interview test. You have already taken the written test and you are now being called for the interview test – the final part of the formal examination.

You may think that it is not possible to prepare for an interview test and that there are no procedures to follow during an interview. Our purpose is to point out some things you can do in advance that will help you and some good rules to follow and pitfalls to avoid while you are being interviewed.

What is an interview supposed to test?

The written examination is designed to test the technical knowledge and competence of the candidate; the oral is designed to evaluate intangible qualities, not readily measured otherwise, and to establish a list showing the relative fitness of each candidate – as measured against his competitors – for the position sought. Scoring is not on the basis of "right" and "wrong," but on a sliding scale of values ranging from "not passable" to "outstanding." As a matter of fact, it is possible to achieve a relatively low score without a single "incorrect" answer because of evident weakness in the qualities being measured.

Occasionally, an examination may consist entirely of an oral test – either an individual or a group oral. In such cases, information is sought concerning the technical knowledges and abilities of the candidate, since there has been no written examination for this purpose. More commonly, however, an oral test is used to supplement a written examination.

Who conducts interviews?

The composition of oral boards varies among different jurisdictions. In nearly all, a representative of the personnel department serves as chairman. One of the members of the board may be a representative of the department in which the candidate would work. In some cases, "outside experts" are used, and, frequently, a businessman or some other representative of the general public is asked to serve. Labor and management or other special groups may be represented. The aim is to secure the services of experts in the appropriate field.

However the board is composed, it is a good idea (and not at all improper or unethical) to ascertain in advance of the interview who the members are and what groups they represent. When you are introduced to them, you will have some idea of their backgrounds and interests, and at least you will not stutter and stammer over their names.

What should be done before the interview?

While knowledge about the board members is useful and takes some of the surprise element out of the interview, there is other preparation which is more substantive. It *is* possible to prepare for an oral interview – in several ways:

1) Keep a copy of your application and review it carefully before the interview

This may be the only document before the oral board, and the starting point of the interview. Know what education and experience you have listed there, and the sequence and dates of all of it. Sometimes the board will ask you to review the highlights of your experience for them; you should not have to hem and haw doing it.

2) Study the class specification and the examination announcement

Usually, the oral board has one or both of these to guide them. The qualities, characteristics or knowledges required by the position sought are stated in these documents. They offer valuable clues as to the nature of the oral interview. For example, if the job involves supervisory responsibilities, the announcement will usually indicate that knowledge of modern supervisory methods and the qualifications of the candidate as a supervisor will be tested. If so, you can expect such questions, frequently in the form of a hypothetical situation which you are expected to solve. NEVER go into an oral without knowledge of the duties and responsibilities of the job you seek.

3) Think through each qualification required

Try to visualize the kind of questions you would ask if you were a board member. How well could you answer them? Try especially to appraise your own knowledge and background in each area, *measured against the job sought*, and identify any areas in which you are weak. Be critical and realistic – do not flatter yourself.

4) Do some general reading in areas in which you feel you may be weak

For example, if the job involves supervision and your past experience has NOT, some general reading in supervisory methods and practices, particularly in the field of human relations, might be useful. Do NOT study agency procedures or detailed manuals. The oral board will be testing your understanding and capacity, not your memory.

5) Get a good night's sleep and watch your general health and mental attitude

You will want a clear head at the interview. Take care of a cold or any other minor ailment, and of course, no hangovers.

What should be done on the day of the interview?

Now comes the day of the interview itself. Give yourself plenty of time to get there. Plan to arrive somewhat ahead of the scheduled time, particularly if your appointment is in the fore part of the day. If a previous candidate fails to appear, the board might be ready for you a bit early. By early afternoon an oral board is almost invariably behind schedule if there are many candidates, and you may have to wait. Take along a book or magazine to read, or your application to review, but leave any extraneous material in the waiting room when you go in for your interview. In any event, relax and compose yourself.

The matter of dress is important. The board is forming impressions about you – from your experience, your manners, your attitude, and your appearance. Give your personal appearance careful attention. Dress your best, but not your flashiest. Choose conservative, appropriate clothing, and be sure it is immaculate. This is a business interview, and your appearance should indicate that you regard it as such. Besides, being well groomed and properly dressed will help boost your confidence.

Sooner or later, someone will call your name and escort you into the interview room. *This is it.* From here on you are on your own. It is too late for any more preparation. But remember, you asked for this opportunity to prove your fitness, and you are here because your request was granted.

What happens when you go in?

The usual sequence of events will be as follows: The clerk (who is often the board stenographer) will introduce you to the chairman of the oral board, who will introduce you to the other members of the board. Acknowledge the introductions before you sit down. Do not be surprised if you find a microphone facing you or a stenotypist sitting by. Oral interviews are usually recorded in the event of an appeal or other review.

Usually the chairman of the board will open the interview by reviewing the highlights of your education and work experience from your application – primarily for the benefit of the other members of the board, as well as to get the material into the record. Do not interrupt or comment unless there is an error or significant misinterpretation; if that is the case, do not hesitate. But do not quibble about insignificant matters. Also, he will usually ask you some question about your education, experience or your present job – partly to get you to start talking and to establish the interviewing "rapport." He may start the actual questioning, or turn it over to one of the other members. Frequently, each member undertakes the questioning on a particular area, one in which he is perhaps most competent, so you can expect each member to participate in the examination. Because time is limited, you may also expect some rather abrupt switches in the direction the questioning takes, so do not be upset by it. Normally, a board member will not pursue a single line of questioning unless he discovers a particular strength or weakness.

After each member has participated, the chairman will usually ask whether any member has any further questions, then will ask you if you have anything you wish to add. Unless you are expecting this question, it may floor you. Worse, it may start you off on an extended, extemporaneous speech. The board is not usually seeking more information. The question is principally to offer you a last opportunity to present further qualifications or to indicate that you have nothing to add. So, if you feel that a significant qualification or characteristic has been overlooked, it is proper to point it out in a sentence or so. Do not compliment the board on the thoroughness of their examination – they have been sketchy, and you know it. If you wish, merely say, "No thank you, I have nothing further to add." This is a point where you can "talk yourself out" of a good impression or fail to present an important bit of information. Remember, *you close the interview yourself.*

The chairman will then say, "That is all, Mr. _____, thank you." Do not be startled; the interview is over, and quicker than you think. Thank him, gather your belongings and take your leave. Save your sigh of relief for the other side of the door.

How to put your best foot forward

Throughout this entire process, you may feel that the board individually and collectively is trying to pierce your defenses, seek out your hidden weaknesses and embarrass and confuse you. Actually, this is not true. They are obliged to make an appraisal of your qualifications for the job you are seeking, and they want to see you in your best light. Remember, they must interview all candidates and a non-cooperative candidate may become a failure in spite of their best efforts to bring out his qualifications. Here are 15 suggestions that will help you:

1) Be natural – Keep your attitude confident, not cocky

If you are not confident that you can do the job, do not expect the board to be. Do not apologize for your weaknesses, try to bring out your strong points. The board is interested in a positive, not negative, presentation. Cockiness will antagonize any board member and make him wonder if you are covering up a weakness by a false show of strength.

2) Get comfortable, but don't lounge or sprawl

Sit erectly but not stiffly. A careless posture may lead the board to conclude that you are careless in other things, or at least that you are not impressed by the importance of the occasion. Either conclusion is natural, even if incorrect. Do not fuss with your clothing, a pencil or an ashtray. Your hands may occasionally be useful to emphasize a point; do not let them become a point of distraction.

3) Do not wisecrack or make small talk

This is a serious situation, and your attitude should show that you consider it as such. Further, the time of the board is limited – they do not want to waste it, and neither should you.

4) Do not exaggerate your experience or abilities

In the first place, from information in the application or other interviews and sources, the board may know more about you than you think. Secondly, you probably will not get away with it. An experienced board is rather adept at spotting such a situation, so do not take the chance.

5) If you know a board member, do not make a point of it, yet do not hide it

Certainly you are not fooling him, and probably not the other members of the board. Do not try to take advantage of your acquaintanceship – it will probably do you little good.

6) Do not dominate the interview

Let the board do that. They will give you the clues – do not assume that you have to do all the talking. Realize that the board has a number of questions to ask you, and do not try to take up all the interview time by showing off your extensive knowledge of the answer to the first one.

7) Be attentive

You only have 20 minutes or so, and you should keep your attention at its sharpest throughout. When a member is addressing a problem or question to you, give him your undivided attention. Address your reply principally to him, but do not exclude the other board members.

8) Do not interrupt

A board member may be stating a problem for you to analyze. He will ask you a question when the time comes. Let him state the problem, and wait for the question.

9) Make sure you understand the question

Do not try to answer until you are sure what the question is. If it is not clear, restate it in your own words or ask the board member to clarify it for you. However, do not haggle about minor elements.

10) Reply promptly but not hastily

A common entry on oral board rating sheets is "candidate responded readily," or "candidate hesitated in replies." Respond as promptly and quickly as you can, but do not jump to a hasty, ill-considered answer.

11) Do not be peremptory in your answers

A brief answer is proper – but do not fire your answer back. That is a losing game from your point of view. The board member can probably ask questions much faster than you can answer them.

12) Do not try to create the answer you think the board member wants

He is interested in what kind of mind you have and how it works – not in playing games. Furthermore, he can usually spot this practice and will actually grade you down on it.

13) Do not switch sides in your reply merely to agree with a board member

Frequently, a member will take a contrary position merely to draw you out and to see if you are willing and able to defend your point of view. Do not start a debate, yet do not surrender a good position. If a position is worth taking, it is worth defending.

14) Do not be afraid to admit an error in judgment if you are shown to be wrong

The board knows that you are forced to reply without any opportunity for careful consideration. Your answer may be demonstrably wrong. If so, admit it and get on with the interview.

15) Do not dwell at length on your present job

The opening question may relate to your present assignment. Answer the question but do not go into an extended discussion. You are being examined for a *new* job, not your present one. As a matter of fact, try to phrase ALL your answers in terms of the job for which you are being examined.

Basis of Rating

Probably you will forget most of these "do's" and "don'ts" when you walk into the oral interview room. Even remembering them all will not ensure you a passing grade. Perhaps you did not have the qualifications in the first place. But remembering them will help you to put your best foot forward, without treading on the toes of the board members.

Rumor and popular opinion to the contrary notwithstanding, an oral board wants you to make the best appearance possible. They know you are under pressure – but they also want to see how you respond to it as a guide to what your reaction would be under the pressures of the job you seek. They will be influenced by the degree of poise you display, the personal traits you show and the manner in which you respond.

ABOUT THIS BOOK

This book contains tests divided into Examination Sections. Go through each test, answering every question in the margin. We have also attached a sample answer sheet at the back of the book that can be removed and used. At the end of each test look at the answer key and check your answers. On the ones you got wrong, look at the right answer choice and learn. Do not fill in the answers first. Do not memorize the questions and answers, but understand the answer and principles involved. On your test, the questions will likely be different from the samples. Questions are changed and new ones added. If you understand these past questions you should have success with any changes that arise. Tests may consist of several types of questions. We have additional books on each subject should more study be advisable or necessary for you. Finally, the more you study, the better prepared you will be. This book is intended to be the last thing you study before you walk into the examination room. Prior study of relevant texts is also recommended. NLC publishes some of these in our Fundamental Series. Knowledge and good sense are important factors in passing your exam. Good luck also helps. So now study this Passbook, absorb the material contained within and take that knowledge into the examination. Then do your best to pass that exam.

EXAMINATION SECTION

EXAMINATION SECTION
TEST 1

DIRECTIONS: Each question or incomplete statement is followed by several suggested answers or completions. Select the one that BEST answers the question or completes the statement. *PRINT THE LETTER OF THE CORRECT ANSWER IN THE SPACE AT THE RIGHT.*

1. The history of the nursing home field, in general, has been tied to 1.____

    A. home health care practitioners
    B. sectarian cooperatives
    C. investor-owned enterprise
    D. not-for-profit public administration

2. Currently, what is the approximate percentage of nursing home admissions that come from hospitals? 2.____

    A. Less than 15   B. 20-30
    C. 30-45   D. More than 50

3. The _____ long-term care facility provides on-site registered nursing supervision for one nursing shift per day. 3.____

    A. skilled nursing   B. intermediate
    C. residential   D. extended

4. In most traditional models, the quality of nursing home care has been measured by _____ variables. 4.____

    A. structural   B. financial
    C. procedural   D. outcome

5. In the 1990s, the type of long-term care facilities which experienced the lowest growth rate were 5.____

    A. nursing facilities
    B. home care agencies
    C. residential care facilities
    D. adult day care agencies

6. The Nursing Home Reform Act of 1987 requires 6.____

    A. at least 12-hour coverage by licensed nursing personnel
    B. at least 12-hour coverage by one or more registered nurses
    C. 24-hour coverage by licensed nursing personnel
    D. 24-hour coverage by one or more registered nurses

7. The input-conversion-output model of health service organizations includes each of the following assumptions EXCEPT 7.____

    A. the organization interacts with, and is affected by, its external environment
    B. the organization is the formal setting in which objectives are accomplished by converting resources

C. managers are the catalysts who cause the conversion of resources into satisfied objectives
D. outputs are obtained from the external environment and inputs go into it

8. Studies indicate that the LEAST common process deficiency occurring in United States nursing homes is

   A. unsanitary environment
   B. improper restraints
   C. a failure to comprehensively assess resident needs
   D. inadequate activities

9. In the past decade or so, the use of gerontological nurse specialists (GNSs) and geriatric nurse practitioners (GNPs) in nursing facilities has generally had each of the following effects EXCEPT

   A. reduced reliance on nursing assistants for direct patient care
   B. improved admission and ongoing patient assessments
   C. reduced use of psychotropic drugs
   D. decreased incontinence

10. In its quarterly scheduling and budgeting meeting, the management team at a nursing home hopes to make an accurate estimate of the time a new activity will require. The team uses the following figures in its estimate: the most optimistic projection is that the activity will take 4 weeks; the most likely time estimate is 6 weeks; and the worst-case projection is that the activity will take 10 weeks.
    According to the standard procedure for making such estimates, the team should figure a period of _____ weeks into its planning and budgeting for this activity.

    A. 4 B. 6 1/3 C. 8 2/3 D. 10

11. The staff at a nursing home has become so overwhelmed with requests for personal meal deliveries that on occasion, some deliveries are not made as scheduled. In brainstorming about the possible explanations why deliveries could not meet demand, the management team decides to survey all relevant staff members and have them rank the reasons in order of importance.
    Which of the following visual tools would best help the team to do this?

    A. Decision grid
    B. Pareto diagram
    C. Payoff table
    D. Ishikawa (fishbone) diagram

12. Which of the following is NOT an attribute that is common to all levels of management in a health care organization such as a nursing home?

    A. Role in formulation of policies which govern the overall philosophy and everyday operations of the organization
    B. Accountability to superiors for results
    C. Formal appointment to a position of authority by the organization
    D. Responsibility for directing work efforts of others

13. Which of the following is LEAST likely to be a characteristic associated with a resident in a nursing facility?   13._____

    A. Contactures
    B. Bowel incontinence
    C. Indwelling catheters
    D. Organic psychiatric conditions

14. Which of the following funding sources accounts for about half of expenditures on nursing home care?   14._____

    A. Out-of-pocket
    B. Medicaid
    C. Medicare
    D. Private insurance

15. Which of the following projections for nursing home industry is probably NOT accurate?   15._____

    A. The expansion of rehabilitative services
    B. A dependence on public and out-of-pocket financing
    C. An increasingly complex case mix
    D. A movement of experienced registered nurses from hospitals to nursing facilities

16. According to the life-cycle model of voluntary inter-organizational relationships, a nursing home in the transition stage would   16._____

    A. seek to sustain member commitment
    B. define purposes of the facility
    C. establish professional evaluation procedures
    D. hire or form a management group

17. In the past decade or so, which of the following types of nursing home patients have shown the most obvious growth in number?   17._____

    A. The terminally ill
    B. Those who use a nursing facility for recovery and rehabilitation following an acute hospital stay
    C. Those with multiple chronic conditions and cognitive and functional impairments who will remain at the facility for the rest of their lives
    D. Those under the age of 65

18. The _____ long-term care facilities is typically part of a general acute hospital.   18._____

    A. skilled nursing
    B. intermediate
    C. residential
    D. extended

19. Which of the following situations or characteristics is most likely to result in a high staff turnover rate at a nursing home?   19._____

    A. Inclusion of nursing assistants as part of care team
    B. Provision of free on-site child care
    C. Minimal use of part-time staff
    D. Low nursing assistant (NA)-to-bed ratios

20. Which of the following is considered a process variable involved in nursing home care?   20._____

    A. Bladder training
    B. Theft/abuse
    C. Depression
    D. Payor mix

21. Which of the following is a presupposition involved with the use of staffing standards or ratios as an indicator of the quality of care in nursing homes?

    A. Fixed staffing-to-resident ratios can be established across all facilities.
    B. Higher staff ratios lead to improved processes and care outcomes.
    C. Facilities should use case-mix methods for adjusting their staffing levels.
    D. Higher staff ratios will lead to greater revenue due to time-saving measures.

22. In general, which of the following is a process of approving a paramedical employee which involves the appropriate professional association, often in addition to the American Medical Association?

    A. Endorsement
    B. Licensure
    C. Certification
    D. Registration

23. Among nursing home residents, the common denominator is

    A. sensory impairment
    B. functional impairment
    C. cognitive impairment
    D. involuntary admission

24. Most of the direct care in the nursing home environment is provided by

    A. licensed practical nurses
    B. registered nurses
    C. nursing assistants
    D. geriatric nurse practitioners

25. Since the mid-1980s, which of the following types of nursing professionals have experienced the greatest percentage increase in nursing homes?

    A. Geriatric nurse practitioners
    B. Nursing assistants
    C. Registered nurses
    D. Licensed practical nurses

26. Which of the following funding sources accounts for about 1/10 of expenditures on nursing home care?

    A. Out-of-pocket
    B. Medicaid
    C. Medicare
    D. Private insurance

27. The irony of most nursing home policies regarding privacy is that often

    A. the most desirable space in a home is awarded to the least desirable resident
    B. they emphasize the privacy of the staff over that of the residents
    C. the only private space available is dedicated to unpleasant procedures
    D. they are subject to restrictive state CON legislation

28. Which agency of the Department of Health and Human Services is responsible for administering the Medicare and Medicaid programs?

    A. Administration on Aging
    B. Public Health Service
    C. Social Security Administration
    D. Health Care Financing Administration (HCFA)

29. Among all nursing facilities nationwide, what is the average number of nursing care hours provided by registered nurses per resident day? 29.____

   A. 0.5   B. 1   C. 1.5   D. 2

30. Which of the following is a cooperative tactic for negotiating with employees? 30.____

   A. Disclosing only the information necessary to support the organization's position
   B. Maximizing solutions that have joint utility
   C. Stating a problem in terms of the organization's preferred solution
   D. Setting specific goals

KEY (CORRECT ANSWERS)

1. C
2. D
3. B
4. A
5. A

6. C
7. D
8. D
9. A
10. B

11. B
12. A
13. C
14. B
15. D

16. D
17. B
18. D
19. D
20. A

21. B
22. C
23. B
24. C
25. D

26. C
27. A
28. D
29. A
30. B

TEST 2

DIRECTIONS: Each question or incomplete statement is followed by several suggested answers or completions. Select the one that BEST answers the question or completes the statement. *PRINT THE LETTER OF THE CORRECT ANSWER IN THE SPACE AT THE RIGHT.*

1. Which of the following was instituted for the first time by the federal nursing home regulations that were part of the Omnibus Budget Reconciliation Act of 1987 (OBRA 87)?   1.____

    A. The right of cognitively lucid residents to choose their own roommates
    B. Guidelines for the use of physical restraints
    C. Restrictions on resident payor mixes
    D. The right of residents to organize and participate in resident councils

2. Which of the following is an element of classical organizational design rather than more recently formulated approaches?   2.____

    A. Centralized decision-making
    B. High and actively sought performance goals
    C. Open, extensive interaction process
    D. Motivational process taps a broad range of motives through participatory methods

3. So far, advance directives in nursing home care have been used primarily as a mechanism for   3.____

    A. limiting the use of restraints
    B. sustaining a desired level of stimulation and personal attention
    C. limiting life-sustaining treatments
    D. screening out undesirable roommates

4. In the field of health care, the effects of the shift from cost-based reimbursement to rate-based payment have generally included each of the following EXCEPT   4.____

    A. a reduction in the overall types of services and procedures
    B. a reduction in the number of diagnostic and therapeutic procedures
    C. the revision of medical protocols
    D. increased efficiency of operation

5. It is possible, in some instances, for a nursing facility to waive certain federal staffing requirements. In such cases, the facility must obtain a waiver   5.____

    A. at the end of each fiscal quarter
    B. every six months
    C. annually
    D. every two years

6. Nursing homes which make extensive use of tube feedings should be aware that the practice increases the risk of each of the following undesirable outcomes EXCEPT   6.____

    A. lung infection   B. tube misplacement
    C. pain   D. weight loss

7. In recent years, the incidence of injuries and illnesses per 100 workers in nursing and personal care homes in the United States has remained at around

   A. 7 B. 15 C. 26 D. 35

8. Which of the following is generally considered to be a DISADVANTAGE associated with an informal organization?

   A. Restrictive channels of communication
   B. Clashes with the formal organization
   C. The manager's job is made more complex
   D. Destabilizing effect on work groups

9. A formal training program for nursing assistants should always

   A. be limited to functional assessments in order to avoid legal problems
   B. be phased out by the end of the first year of employment
   C. include sensitivity training
   D. be implemented by non-nursing personnel

10. A nursing home director is faced with a 60% probability that the demand for a certain service will increase by 20% next year, and a 40% probability that demand for the service will increase by 10%. The decision is whether to hire another staff member to handle the increased demand, or let the existing staff devise a way to handle the increased demand. Which of the following visual elements might help the director to make this choice?

    A. Ishikawa (fishbone) diagram
    B. Pareto diagram
    C. Nomograph
    D. Decision tree

11. Which of the following factors is currently LEAST likely to affect the demand for nursing home services?

    A. The projected growth of the older population
    B. An increase in the transfer of medical technology to nursing homes
    C. A decrease in the range of services offered
    D. Recent government policy changes

12. An effect of the federal regulations that were issued in 1990 is that state surveys were

    A. redesigned to include financial incentives for quality care
    B. required upon both admission and discharge
    C. required at the end of each fiscal quarter
    D. redesigned to be more outcome-oriented

13. Which of the following is a federal agency with regulatory power over the operations of nursing homes?

    A. American College of Health Executives (ACHE)
    B. Joint Commission on the Accreditation of Health Care Organizations (JCAHO)
    C. Accrediting Commission on Education for Health Services Administration (ACE-HSA)
    D. Health Care Finance Administration (HCFA)

14. Studies indicate that the MOST common outcome deficiency occurring in United States nursing homes is

    A. a failure to maintain the dignity of residents
    B. the inadequate treatment of incontinence
    C. the inadequate treatment of pressure sores
    D. an excessive mortality rate

15. Currently, the most important federal policy affecting the supply of long-term care beds is

    A. social regulations such as those issued by OSHA
    B. state CON legislation
    C. Medicaid reimbursement policy
    D. Medicare reimbursement policy

16. In today's health care market, the main reason most clients prefer subacute care over hospital care is because

    A. the quality of clinical care is much higher
    B. there is a greater emphasis on rehabilitative services
    C. overall costs are much lower
    D. the quality of therapeutic care is much higher

17. Which of the following payers is/are usually involved in cost-based reimbursement programs?
    I. Medicare
    II. Medicaid
    III. Blue Cross
    IV. Commercial third-party insurer

    The CORRECT answer is:

    A. I only   B. I, II   C. II, III   D. III, IV

18. Approximately what percentage of nursing home residents are discharged from a facility within 3 months of admission?

    A. Fewer than 10
    B. 15
    C. 35
    D. More than 50

19. Recent studies of physical restraints in nursing homes have generally indicated that they
    I. are generally used only when the safety of a resident is threatened
    II. are an effective means of correcting undesirable resident behaviors
    III. tend to increase overall costs to a nursing facility
    IV. are generally overused

    The CORRECT answer is:

    A. I only   B. I, II   C. II, III   D. III, IV

20. In general, nursing home managers who seek to increase the autonomy of residents in their facility should begin by focusing critical attention on the

    A. schedule of activities
    B. staff-resident relationship
    C. amount of space set aside for individual privacy
    D. means by which roommates are selected

21. The Omnibus Budget Reconciliation Act of 1987 (OBRA 87) provided each of the following as a federal requirement of nursing homes EXCEPT

    A. a director of nursing who is a registered nurse
    B. a registered nurse on duty at least 8 hours a day
    C. an administrator who is a registered nurse
    D. licensed nurses on duty 24 hours a day

22. In the nationwide distribution of all health care expenditures, nursing home care accounts for about _____ %.

    A. 7   B. 12   C. 22   D. 41

23. Most federal nursing home regulations, especially those issued more than ten years ago, have focused on

    A. civil rights   B. quality of life
    C. safety   D. the reimbursement process

24. Which of the following is NOT a generalized trend among nursing assistants employed in United States nursing homes?

    A. About three-fourths have not completed high school
    B. About two-thirds are women
    C. They often come from low-income families
    D. Less than half have any employer-based health insurance coverage

25. Currently, the turnover rate among directors of nursing at United States nursing facilities is about _____ %.

    A. 5   B. 15   C. 35   D. 55

26. Which of the following is NOT generally considered a component of the controlling function in health care organizations?

    A. Developing and improving accounting and budgeting practices
    B. Containing costs of professional services to patients
    C. Motivating, advising, and counseling management personnel
    D. Improving the accessibility of patient care services

27. Which of the following is most likely to be ranked as the top priority among nursing home residents?

    A. Ability to leave the facility for outings
    B. Roommates
    C. Quality of care
    D. Food

28. The management team at a nursing home is at a point in the development of its operations that stakeholders are beginning to receive benefits from their previous investments. According to the life-cycle model of interorganizational relationships, this facility is in the _____ stage.

    A. emergence   B. transition
    C. critical crossroads   D. maturity

29. Which of the following is considered a structural variable involved in nursing home care?

   A. Sanitation
   B. Urinary incontinence
   C. Patient satisfaction
   D. Accreditation

30. According to the life-cycle model of voluntary interorganizational relationships, a nursing home in the maturity stage would

   A. seek to motivate employees to achieve the purposes of the facility
   B. manage decisions about the future of the facility
   C. develop criteria for admission
   D. establish mechanisms for coordination and control

KEY (CORRECT ANSWERS)

1.	D	16.	C
2.	A	17.	C
3.	C	18.	D
4.	A	19.	D
5.	C	20.	B
6.	D	21.	C
7.	B	22.	A
8.	B	23.	C
9.	C	24.	B
10.	D	25.	C
11.	C	26.	C
12.	D	27.	A
13.	D	28.	C
14.	A	29.	D
15.	B	30.	B

EXAMINATION SECTION
TEST 1

DIRECTIONS: Each question or incomplete statement is followed by several suggested answers or completions. Select the one that BEST answers the question or completes the statement. *PRINT THE LETTER OF THE CORRECT ANSWER IN THE SPACE AT THE RIGHT.*

1. In evaluating the timing *of* an activity and sequencing the alternatives, a management team at a nursing home should determine the *critical path* through the nursing home's network. The critical path in this context is the element of the activity which

    A. takes the longest to complete
    B. takes the shortest time to complete
    C. requires the most resources
    D. requires the fewest resources

2. Which of the following most accurately states the growing trend in the structuring of the nursing home industry?

    A. Greater proportional reliance on public financing
    B. Consolidation into larger health care organizations
    C. Greater reliance on extended-care facilities
    D. Dispersement into smaller community-level facilities

3. According to most health care professionals and executives, the most ethically troubling aspects of the Medicaid program is that

    A. recipients must prove their eligibility in accord with the program's provisions
    B. many elderly transfer their assets to children in order to make themselves eligible
    C. taxes from working people are used to provide services to elderly beneficiaries
    D. states are subject to federal regulations in the apportionment of benefits

4. Studies of nursing homes have generally indicated that a low percentage of private-pay patients in a nursing facility

    A. is a negative indicator of the quality of care
    B. more typically occurs in urban facilities
    C. usually leads to a greater reliance on physical restraints
    D. may increase the degree to which a facility is subject to federal regulation

5. Which of the following payors is/are usually involved in fixed reimbursement programs?
    I. Medicare
    II. Medicaid
    III. Blue Cross
    IV. Commercial third-party insurer

    The CORRECT answer is:

    A. I, II
    B. I, III
    C. II, III, IV
    D. II, IV

6. Studies indicate that the MOST common process deficiency in United States nursing homes is

   A. an inadequate care plan
   B. a hazardous environment
   C. unsanitary food
   D. the improper use of restraints

7. The effect of the prospective payment system for Medicare, established in 1983, was to

   A. provide a cost-based approach to reimbursement
   B. establish fixed rates for each Medicare admission by diagnosis
   C. regulate the way in which long-term care institutions competed against each other for market share
   D. establish a new system of organizational review for all health care institutions

8. Most staff experience has shown that the activity with which residents are most likely to need assistance is

   A. eating
   B. dressing
   C. getting in or out of a chair
   D. bathing

9. Federal regulations require nursing facilities to complete minimum data set (MDS) forms for patients within _____ of admission.

   A. 48 hours   B. 14 days   C. 30 days   D. 3 months

10. In most nursing homes, daily life is permeated by a model of staff-resident relationships that is most clearly drawn from

    A. child-care settings
    B. client-centered professions such as law
    C. acute-care medical settings
    D. municipal government and constituents

11. Which of the following were effects of the 1983 introduction of Medicare's Prospective Payment System (PPS)?

    I. Overall decreases in long-term care costs
    II. More flexibility in long-term care reimbursement procedures
    III. More referrals and admissions to nursing facilities
    IV. Early discharge from acute care facilities

    The CORRECT answer is:

    A. I, II   B. II, III   C. III, IV   D. I, IV

12. Nationwide, what is the average total number of nursing care hours per resident day in Medicaid-only facilities?

    A. 1   B. 2   C. 3   D. 4

13. Which of the qualitative techniques for decision analysis attempts to optimize the distribution of scarce resources among competing activities?

    A. Queuing theory
    B. Regression analysis
    C. Linear programming
    D. Network analysis

14. How many hours of in-service training for nursing assistants is currently required each year by federal regulations?

    A. 0   B. 12   C. 40   D. 64

15. Which of the following is NOT a trend currently taking place in the demographics of United States health care clients?

    A. Increasing poverty
    B. A rapidly changing racial and ethnic composition due to immigration and growing minority populations
    C. A trend toward smaller family size
    D. An increase in the percentage of younger clients

16. Which of the following factors are affected by the patient mix at a nursing home?
    I. Staffing
    II. Service mix
    III. The way in which quality-of-care indicators should be interpreted
    IV. Regulations affecting nursing home activities and staffing
    The CORRECT answer is:

    A. I, II
    B. II, IV
    C. I, II, III
    D. I, III

17. Which of the following is a difference between professional review organizations (PROs) and the older professional standards review organizations (PSROs) established by federal health care regulations?

    A. PROs are made up of solely not-for-profit, physician-sponsored groups.
    B. PROs are paid by federal grants.
    C. PSROs involve smaller geographic areas.
    D. PSROs were subject to the Freedom of Information Act (FOIA)

18. A nursing home administrator or director of nursing at a nursing home can expect the leading cause of illness or injury among nursing assistants to be

    A. strains and sprains, mostly involving the back
    B. slips or falls to a lower level
    C. respiratory infection
    D. needlestick injuries

19. The largest association for long-term care facilities in the United States is the

    A. Group Health Association of America (GHAA)
    B. American Hospital Association (AHA)
    C. Federation of American Hospitals (FAH)
    D. American Health Care Association (AHCA)

20. Of the following aspects of nursing home life, the one most exclusively characteristic of United States facilities is the

    A. housing of residents in shared rooms
    B. degree to which physical and chemical restraints are used
    C. use of geriatric or gerontological nursing staff
    D. attempt to involve family members in formulating a care plan

21. Overall, out-of-pocket contributions from clients now accounts for about _____ % of all expenditures on nursing home care in the United States.

    A. 11   B. 22   C. 33   D. 44

22. Compared to nonprofit nursing homes, for-profit facilities generally tend to

    A. have substantially fewer staff
    B. provide better quality care to Medicaid beneficiaries and self-pay residents
    C. have fewer adverse outcomes from pressure sores
    D. make substantially greater use of physical restraints

23. Which of the following is an element of the bureaucratic model of management?

    A. Interdepartmental collaboration
    B. Positions arranged in a matrix
    C. Generalization of tasks
    D. A consistent system of abstract rules

24. Which of the following is the professional society to which a nursing home executive would belong?

    A. American College of Health Executives (ACHE)
    B. American Health Care Administration (AHCA)
    C. Accrediting Commission on Education for Health Services Administration (ACE-HSA)
    D. American Public Health Administration (APHA)

25. Of the following generalizations about nursing home residents, the CORRECT one is that about

    A. 75% are female
    B. 20% are chairbound
    C. 75% are bladder incontinent
    D. 20% require tube feeding

26. The types of managerial decisions made at organizations such as health care facilities typically include each of the following EXCEPT

    A. programmed-nonprogrammed
    B. inclusive-exclusive
    C. administrative-operational
    D. ends-means

27. Gerontological nurse specialists (GNSs) and geriatric nurse practitioners (GNPs) can improve resident outcomes in nursing facilities by
    I. increasing the ability of a facility to care for more complex and acutely ill patients
    II. reducing the use of hospital services
    III. changing the focus from custodial to rehabilitative care
    IV. reducing the incidence of resident behaviors requiring physical restraint
    The CORRECT answer is:

    A. I, II
    B. II, III
    C. III, IV
    D. I, II, III, IV

27.____

28. Studies indicate that the LEAST common outcome deficiency in United States nursing homes is

    A. poor nutrition
    B. resident abuse
    C. failure to prevent pressure sores
    D. inadequate treatment of incontinence

28.____

29. Nursing homes which make extensive use of urinary catheters should be aware that the practice increases the risk of each of the following undesirable outcomes EXCEPT

    A. abscesses
    B. urinary tract infection
    C. malnutrition
    D. renal failure

29.____

30. Programs for cognitively impaired residents in nursing homes should include
    I. music
    II. space set aside where movements will not disturb others
    III. periods of unstructured activity
    IV. small, confined spaces
    The CORRECT answer is:

    A. I, II
    B. II, III
    C. III, IV
    D. I, IV

30.____

KEY (CORRECT ANSWERS)

1.	A	16.	C
2.	B	17.	C
3.	B	18.	A
4.	A	19.	D
5.	B	20.	B
6.	C	21.	C
7.	B	22.	B
8.	D	23.	D
9.	B	24.	A
10.	C	25.	A
11.	C	26.	B
12.	C	27.	D
13.	C	28.	B
14.	B	29.	C
15.	D	30.	A

TEST 2

DIRECTIONS: Each question or incomplete statement is followed by several suggested answers or completions. Select the one that BEST answers the question or completes the statement. *PRINT THE LETTER OF THE CORRECT ANSWER IN THE SPACE AT THE RIGHT.*

1. Which of the following is NOT a provision of the Omnibus Budget Reconciliation Act of 1987 (OBRA 87)? 1.____

    A. Nursing homes were encouraged to shift the focus of care from custodial to rehabilitative care.
    B. State Medicaid programs were encouraged to adjust their rates.
    C. Nursing homes were encouraged to develop a resident assessment program for every patient upon discharge.
    D. Nursing homes receiving federal funds were required to ensure a high quality of life in addition to a high quality of care.

2. Which of the following is an element of a *functional* organization, as opposed to a *project* organization? 2.____

    A. Superior-subordinate boundaries are less clear.
    B. Line functions have direct responsibility for accomplishing objectives.
    C. Prime emphasis is placed on horizontal and diagonal work flow.
    D. Management is a joint venture of many relatively independent organizations.

3. Which of the demographic sectors is most clearly on the increase among nursing home residents? 3.____

    A. Males
    B. Those over the age of 85
    C. Those with chronic cognitive impairment
    D. Married couples

4. Since 1988, which of the following types of nursing professionals have experienced the smallest percentage increase in nursing homes? 4.____

    A. Geriatric nurse practitioners
    B. Nursing assistants
    C. Registered nurses
    D. Licensed practical nurses

5. Which of the following is NOT typically a difficulty involved in the use of surrogate decision-makers for cognitively impaired residents? 5.____

    A. The lack of a formally appointed guardian but several de facto guardians
    B. Illegal or unethical decisions made by a guardian
    C. Difficulty in reversing guardianships once cognitive functions are regained
    D. Difficulty in delineating the scope of decision-making for a guardian

6. Which of the following reasons best explains why many nursing home administrators are reluctant to invest in the training of nursing assistants?

   A. Extensive use of part-time staff
   B. High turnover rates
   C. Adequate supervision and instruction by supervising nurses
   D. High nursing assistant-to-bed ratio

7. Which of the following management roles pertains to the effort to establish suitable organizational objectives and to implement plans capable of accomplishing them?

   A. Decisional
   B. Strategist
   C. Informational
   D. Designer

8. Which of the qualitative techniques for decision analysis derives a mathematical equation to describe or express the relationship between the data of two or more variables over a period of time?

   A. Queuing theory
   B. Regression analysis
   C. Linear programming
   D. Network analysis

9. Which of the following is MOST likely to be a characteristic associated with a resident in a nursing facility?

   A. Receiving psychoactive medications
   B. Physical restraints
   C. Bladder incontinence
   D. Bedfast

10. Which of the following are acceptable means by which the staff at a nursing facility can assure respect for the autonomy of cognitively impaired residents?
    I. Advance directives
    II. Asking residents for permission before performing any procedure
    III. Surrogate decision makers
    IV. The use of restraints to insure safety

    The CORRECT answer is:

    A. I only
    B. II, IV
    C. I, III
    D. II, III

11. In cases where the use of physical and chemical restraints are an issue for a resident, the course of action is usually dictated by

    A. the will of the resident's family
    B. the will of the resident
    C. the judgment of the nursing staff
    D. state regulations

12. Which of the following comparisons of fee-for-service (FFS) and managed care (HMO) nursing care is generally TRUE?

    A. Managed care enrollees are more satisfied with their paperwork requirements.
    B. FFS enrollees are more satisfied with their plan's cost.
    C. Managed care enrollees make greater use of their plan's services.
    D. FFS enrollees are less satisfied with their quality of care.

13. Though advance directives have proven helpful in some cases involving the care of cognitively impaired residents, the practice suffers from the significant difficulty of   13.____

    A. compliance with federal and state regulations
    B. frequent conflicts with the facility's formal care policies
    C. family members who step in after the fact to combat the carrying-out of directives
    D. delineating the areas of decision for which advance directives should have force

14. Each of the following is considered to be an element of the internal management function of a nursing home administrator EXCEPT   14.____

    A. evaluating, training, and developing management personnel
    B. developing and improving management information systems
    C. determining and establishing priorities for new services
    D. defining the general course and goal priorities for the organization

15. The current Medicaid floor for a resident's personal-needs allowance is   15.____

    A. $30 a month   B. $75 a month
    C. $1,000 a year   D. $3,000 a year

16. The 1987 Nursing Home Reform Act provides that nursing assistants must be certified and that they must receive _____ hours of training within the first _____ months of employment in order to be certified.   16.____

    A. 10; 2   B. 40; 2   C. 75; 4   D. 120; 4

17. Approximately what percentage of skilled-nursing facilities in the United States have 24-hour coverage by at least one registered nurse?   17.____

    A. 30   B. 50   C. 70   D. 85

18. The staff at a nursing home has become so overwhelmed with requests for IV feedings that it has to postpone several scheduled sessions. In brainstorming about the possible reasons why feedings could not meet demand, the management team decides to first list all the possible explanations.
    Which of the following visual tools would best help the team to do this?   18.____

    A. Decision tree
    B. Pareto diagram
    C. Payoff table
    D. Ishikawa (fishbone) diagram

19. According to many staff surveys, the main problem associated with the federal nursing home regulations issued by the Omnibus Budget Reconciliation Act of 1987 (OBRA 87) is that   19.____

    A. they focus too much on the rehabilitative aspects of care
    B. the time involved in satisfying documentation requirements detracts from the quality of care
    C. the costs of satisfying staffing requirements decrease the likelihood of profitability
    D. they set an unrealistic standard of care for nursing staff

20. In the 1990s, the type of long-term care facilities which experienced the highest growth rate were

   A. nursing facilities
   B. home care agencies
   C. residential care facilities
   D. adult day care agencies

21. Which of the following is considered an outcome variable involved in nursing home care?

   A. Assessment frequency and completeness
   B. Mortality
   C. Use of restraints
   D. Staffing mix

22. The factor which most clearly distinguishes the long-term care market from the hospital market is the

   A. role of private insurance and Medicare
   B. financial status of the clients who utilize services
   C. demand for services
   D. impact of public welfare on expenditures

23. The *second generation* of federal nursing home regulations, issued during the 1990s, tended to focus primarily on

   A. discriminatory admission practices
   B. resident autonomy and respect for rights
   C. safety
   D. reimbursement

24. The purpose of CON legislation, passed in nearly all states by 1983, was to

   A. regulate the amounts charged by health care facilities
   B. divide professional review organizations into their geographic areas of jurisdiction
   C. provide all nonprofessional and paramedical workers in health care organizations with the same workplace hazard protections as doctors and nurses
   D. force institutional health care providers to obtain state approval for construction or renovation projects beyond a certain cost

25. Which of the following is a likely consequence of the shortage of available nursing home care in many states?

   A. More flexible CON requirements at the state level
   B. Greater selectivity in nursing home admission practices
   C. An increasing focus on the individuals with the greatest need for services
   D. An increase in extended care facilities

KEY (CORRECT ANSWERS)

1. C
2. B
3. B
4. B
5. B

6. B
7. B
8. B
9. C
10. C

11. A
12. A
13. D
14. C
15. A

16. C
17. B
18. D
19. B
20. C

21. B
22. A
23. B
24. D
25. B

EXAMINATION SECTION
TEST 1

DIRECTIONS: Each question or incomplete statement is followed by several suggested answers or completions. Select the one that BEST answers the question or completes the statement. *PRINT THE LETTER OF THE CORRECT ANSWER IN THE SPACE AT THE RIGHT.*

1. When developing a conceptual framework for nursing practice with the elderly, a nurse should resolve the question: What

    A. assumptions, beliefs, and values about nursing and the elderly influence my practice?
    B. is the range of expected health outcomes for older persons?
    C. is the nature of the professional nurse's relationship with other health care providers of the elderly?
    D. all of the above

2. Much of gerontological nursing is application of nursing processes and methods, with special attention to the unique influences of the aging process on health and illness. Modifications in elements of nursing practice because patients are of advanced age include all of the following EXCEPT

    A. fast pace of nursing process
    B. attention to the effects of the aging process on disease presentation and responses to disease and treatment
    C. increased alertness for signs of an intensified stress state
    D. financial resources available to implement plan of care

3. Dryness, wrinkling, laxity, uneven pigmentation, and a variety of proliferative lesions of the skin are due to normal aging, the genetic makeup of the individual, and environmental factors, such as sun exposure.
   Lichenification is classified as nonpathologic skin lesions found in the elderly and characterized by

    A. well-circumscribed areas of cutaneous thickening and hardening
    B. results from repeated rubbing or scratching
    C. both of the above
    D. none of the above

4. An estimated 40% of Americans 65-74 years of age suffer from a skin disease that is severe enough for them to seek treatment.
   All of the following are common pathological skin lesions found in the elderly EXCEPT

    A. psoriasis
    B. seborrheic keratoses
    C. herpes zoster
    D. bullous pemphigoid

5. The incidence of potentially blinding diseases increases dramatically after the age of 65. The one of the following that is NOT among the leading causes of blindness in elderly people is

    A. senile macular degeneration
    B. senile angioma (cherry spot)
    C. senile cataract
    D. acute angle closure glaucoma

6. Breast cancer is the most common malignancy found in women and accounts for 2% of deaths in women over 75 years of age.
The BEST diagnostic procedure for breast screening in a woman over 50 years of age includes

   A. breast self-examination
   B. annual professional examination
   C. mammogram
   D. all of the above

7. The aging gut may be characterized by decreased secretions, absorption, and motility. Of the following, the LEAST likely cause of severe abdominal pain is

   A. gallbladder disease, secondary to inflammation, obstruction, or cancer
   B. acute pancreatitis
   C. torsion of testis
   D. mesenteric thrombosis, infarction, or hemorrhage

8. The prevalence of colorectal cancer increases at 40-50 years of age, doubles every 10 years thereafter, and peaks at 75-80 years.
Besides colorectal cancer, other causes of blood in stool includes

   A. hemorrhoids B. fissures
   C. vascular ectasias D. all of the above

9. Within the field of geriatrics, there is an unusually-high probability that nurses will function in a multi-disciplinary approach in providing health care to patients, families and groups of elderly persons. Nurses who work in situations in which they must assume multidisciplinary functions need to

   A. be well-grounded as specialists in geriatrics and gerontology, in the knowledge of normal aging and in the areas of high-risk health problems among the elderly
   B. be visible to consumers, colleagues, and administrators in their nursing roles
   C. offer consultations and expect consultations and referrals on nursing problems
   D. all of the above

10. Persons at greater risk for adverse drug effects include all of the following EXCEPT those who are

    A. of extremely tall stature
    B. 75 years old or older
    C. receiving an excessive number of medications
    D. having renal dysfunction

11. The pharmacist will focus on the names and kinds of drugs being taken.
The nurse will look at some different dimensions, including

    A. previous patterns of utilization of medications
    B. attitudes towards medications and their effects, side effects, and allergies
    C. ethnic or religious influences on the treatment of illness and health maintenance
    D. all of the above

12. Barbiturates, benzodiazepines, and miscellaneous sedative and hypnotic agents comprise another group of drugs overused by the elderly.
    Barbiturates are to be avoided in the elderly because of all of the following risks, EXCEPT

    A. high potential for addiction
    B. hallucinations and delusions
    C. paradoxical agitation
    D. sedation and ataxia

13. Drugs such as chlorpromazine, thioridazine, haloperidol, and thiothixene are often overused by the elderly. Their continual use may cause

    A. extra-pyramidal symptoms such as drug-induced Parkinsonism
    B. tardive dyskinesia
    C. both of the above
    D. none of the above

14. Adequate nursing knowledge is one key to effectiveness in managing a medication regimen.
    For each drug, certain data is needed, but it is NOT necessary for the nurse to know

    A. the purpose of the medication, its function, and the disease or condition for which it is prescribed
    B. the generic and brand names of the medication, its color, and the size and shape of dosage form
    C. detailed information about the company who is manufacturing the drug
    D. the route of administration, e.g., by mouth, inhalation, intravenous, etc.

15. Which of the following questions should the nurse be able to answer for a discharging patient regarding the storage of a drug?

    A. Does the medication need to be refrigerated?
    B. Should it always be left in the original container?
    C. Does this medication have an especially short shelf life?
    D. All of the above

16. Professional health care providers, especially those providing nursing or rehabilitative patient care, should be competent enough in the practice of oral health maintenance to do all of the following EXCEPT

    A. perform gastric endoscopy routinely to rule out GI-related causes or bad oral health
    B. assess oral health status
    C. manage oral hygiene
    D. integrate oral health maintenance into patient care plan

17. A major responsibility in direct nursing care is to prevent progressive oral dysfunction syndrome.
    The classic and common example of PODS may be found in the institutionalized stroke patient who, after a year of post-stroke health care, displays all of the following characteristics EXCEPT

A. inability to cleanse mouth adequately caused by loss of motor skills for oral hygiene
B. inadequate control of dental plaque with rampant tooth decay and advanced periodontal disease
C. oral problems that are extremely resistant to drug treatment and keep on deteriorating
D. progressive loss of self-esteem due to poor esthetics and a noticeable offensive odor from the mouth

18. Dentures are not necessarily used to sustain life, although many patients will not eat appropriately or socialize when their teeth are out of their mouths. Common denture problems often managed by nursing intervention do NOT include 18.____

    A. mixed-up or lost dentures
    B. maintaining good hygiene of dentures to prevent caries or plaque
    C. ill-fitting dentures
    D. broken or poorly functioning dentures

19. Regarding oral health, the nurse who cares for an older person over a period of time should know the 19.____

    A. skills and resources employed to maintain oral health and those being avoided or used ineffectively
    B. patterns in lifestyle that are barriers to oral health, e.g., mouth care, lack of professional care, diet, fluids, and smoking
    C. planning and skills associated with patient's self-care of specific problems, such as protecting damaged or friable oral tissue, dry mouth, bad smell, and so forth
    D. locating resources for professional dental care needs

20. Nurses should routinely evaluate the effectiveness of the oral health practices being performed by persons in their charge. 20.____
    When a mouth has been cleansed daily over a period of time, it should have all of the following characteristics EXCEPT

    A. dental plaque should not be apparent on teeth
    B. tissues should be extremely smooth around the teeth
    C. patient should appreciate the feeling of a clean mouth
    D. there should be no bleeding when brushing or flossing

21. When dental personnel enter an institutional situation, they should 21.____

    A. write all findings, plans, and notes in the chart, with oral hygiene measures specifically written
    B. assist in the training and assessment of oral health maintenance
    C. both of the above
    D. none of the above

22. Each patient needs his own toothbrush, either hand or electric. 22.____
    A nurse should NOT recommend a toothbrush with

    A. curved handle and brushing surfaces
    B. soft nylon bristles
    C. bristle part small enough to reach all areas of mouth easily

D. straight handle and flat brushing surface

23. Recommended care of a toothbrush involves all of the following points EXCEPT: 23.____

   A. Rinse the toothbrush with clean, cold water, and use it to remove any retained food and toothpaste
   B. Store the toothbrush in a dark, airtight place
   C. Use an empty water glass or toothbrush holder to store the toothbrush
   D. Replace the toothbrush when the bristles become loose, bent, broken, or worn

24. Electric toothbrushes may be as effective as hand toothbrushes in maintaining cleanliness of the mouth.   24.____
The recommended method of toothbrushing with an electric toothbrush is to

   A. wet the bristles of the toothbrush with water and place a small amount of dentifrice on them
   B. hold the bristles of the brush lightly against the side of the teeth so that both the teeth and gums are cleaned
   C. brush the tongue side as well as the cheek side of the teeth
   D. all of the above

KEY (CORRECT ANSWERS)

1. D		11. D	
2. A		12. B	
3. C		13. C	
4. B		14. C	
5. B		15. D	
6. D		16. A	
7. C		17. C	
8. D		18. B	
9. D		19. D	
10. A		20. B	

21. B
22. C
23. A
24. B
25. D

TEST 2

DIRECTIONS: Each question or incomplete statement is followed by several suggested answers or completions. Select the one that BEST answers the question or completes the statement. *PRINT THE LETTER OF THE CORRECT ANSWER IN THE SPACE AT THE RIGHT.*

1. Old people are susceptible to many of the diseases of younger adults. Studies of pattern of disease in the United States reveals that the major categories of diseases in elderly people require that special considerations include diseases

    A. that occur to varying degrees in all aged persons, such as atherosclerosis or cataracts
    B. with increased incidence in those of advanced age but not occurring universally, e.g., neoplastic disease, diabetes mellitus, and some dementing disorders
    C. that have more serious consequences in the elderly because of their reduced ability to maintain homeostasis, for example pneumonia, influenza, and trauma
    D. all of the above

1.___

2. A screening profile of individuals at high risk for family mediated abuse or neglect includes all of the following elders EXCEPT those who

    A. live at home and whose needs exceed or soon will exceed their families' ability to meet them
    B. have primary caretakers who are expressing interest and sympathy in dealing with care needs
    C. live in families with a norm of family violence
    D. abuse drugs or alcohol or live with family members who abuse drugs or alcohol or have episodes of loss of control

2.___

3. Constipation is known to occur in at least 25% of older patients, and many reasons have been cited as potentially influential.
NOT included among the factors believed to be contributory is

    A. increase in fluid intake
    B. lack of fiber in the diet to stimulate peristalsis
    C. blunting or loss of the defecation reflex as a consequence of neglect of the urge to defecate
    D. lack of exercise

3.___

4. Oral health maintenance implies that the nurse provide

    A. daily oral hygiene as part of the total patient nursing care
    B. assessment of the mouth at intervals of time appropriate to the patient's health status and his ability to care for himself
    C. advocacy linkage to dental care when problems are detected
    D. all of the above

4.___

5. For millions of Americans over age 65, osteoporosis is a debilitating disease that reduces their mobility and independence.
Factors thought to increase net bone losses of calcium include all of the following EXCEPT

5.___

A. inadequate dietary intake of calcium and vitamin D
B. smoking and excessive alcohol and caffeine consumption
C. excessive physical activity
D. excessive dietary intake of phosphorus and proteins

6. Foods and fluids that aid in the prevention and management of constipation include 6.____

   A. raw vegetables and fruits
   B. at least 6 glasses of water per day
   C. whole grain cereal products
   D. all of the above

7. Suggested treatment and treatment combinations in a woman with post-menopausal osteoporosis include all of the following EXCEPT 7.____

   A. discourage exercise and advise complete bed rest
   B. assure an adequate supply of calcium and vitamin D plus sunlight exposure
   C. take anabolic steroids and estrogen/progestrin combinations as directed by physician
   D. supplement fluoride, especially in areas where water sources are low

8. The physiological, psychological, social, and economic changes that occur in aging people may result in a pattern of living which causes malnutrition and further physical and mental deterioration! for example, they 8.____

   A. cannot afford to do so
   B. have limited mobility which may impair their capacity to shop and cook for themselves
   C. have feelings of rejection and loneliness which obliterate the incentive necessary to prepare and eat a meal alone
   D. all of the above

9. If effective learning is to take place, the instructor must stimulate an interest in the subject of nutrition. It is NOT advisable for a person eating alone to 9.____

   A. set an attractive table, i.e., make meals an event
   B. never watch TV or listen to the radio while eating
   C. eat outdoors when the weather allows
   D. invite guests often for a potluck or meal exchange

10. Special facets of the federally supported nutrition demonstrating-research projects are basic to the success that many of these projects have appreciated.
    Among the supplemental provisions are 10.____

    A. auxiliary services, such as transportation, dental care, and counseling on individual dietary requirements to make it possible for older people to use services
    B. social settings designated for personal adjustment and adequacy of diet
    C. settings conducive to eating meals with others
    D. all of the above

11. Not all primary caregivers experience difficulties in their daily living associated with providing care to the elderly, dependent relatives in their families. Factors increasing the risk of problems in daily living include all of the following EXCEPT 11.____

A. lack of community resources
B. adequate income
C. environmental barriers, such as transportation and housing
D. substance abuse

12. When the demands on primary caregivers and other family members are seen to exceed their resources and disrupt their daily living, emotional responses normally occur. The nurse's role is to help family members

    A. recognize and accept their emotional responses to the situation
    B. accept their responses as abnormal and illegitimate
    C. both of the above
    D. none of the above

13. Restoration or maintenance of balance in a family may require an interdisciplinary team. It becomes important that one member of that team be identified as the coordinator responsible for the case management.
    This individual has a responsibility to

    A. coordinate services and conduct case conferences
    B. keep team members informed about the care plans
    C. conduct ongoing evaluations and updates of the evaluation plans
    D. all of the above

14. Delirium is a common condition, particularly in the hospital setting, and is most often a manifestation of serious systemic disease or an abnormal response to treatment. Diagnostic criteria of delirium includes all of the following EXCEPT

    A. clouding of consciousness
    B. loss of intellectual abilities of sufficient severity to interfere with social or occupational functioning
    C. clinical features that develop over a short period of time and tend to fluctuate over the course of the day
    D. disorientation and memory impairment

15. Dementias are actually a group of diseases sharing a gradual onset, global decline in intellectual capacity and performance, and progressive social incapacitation. The one of the following that is NOT a type of primary dementia is

    A. primary degenerative dementia (Alzheimer's disease)
    B. multi-infarct dementia
    C. Parkinson's dementia
    D. Pick's disease

16. Dementia is an ancient term taken from Latin and literally means *out of one's mind.* Diagnostic criteria for dementia include all of the following EXCEPT

    A. loss of intellectual abilities of sufficient severity to interfere with social or occupational functioning
    B. clouding of consciousness
    C. memory impairment
    D. impaired judgment

17. Nurses may feel some diagnostic confusion between delirium and dementia. Of the following, the feature that favors the diagnosis of dementia is:

    A. Onset of disease is rapid and duration of disease is hours to weeks
    B. Awareness is always impaired
    C. Course of disease is relatively stable
    D. Physical illness or drug toxicity is usually present

18. An older man is on MAO inhibitors for depressive disorder. The nurse should restrict all of the following foods to avoid hypertensive disorder EXCEPT

    A. old cheese
    B. chocolate
    C. white meat
    D. red wines

19. Agitation and restlessness are two of the most pressing behavioral problems that create difficulties in managing everyday living.
    Deterioration is LEAST likely to occur

    A. during periods of fatigue
    B. during early morning hours
    C. following ingestion of certain medications, e.g., indomethacin, pentazocin, and phenytoin, etc.
    D. when infections are present

20. Daily living is MOST likely to be compromised in the presence of agitation and restlessness when those around the agitated person

    A. cannot tolerate the behavior
    B. understand the phenomenon
    C. have workable strategies for dealing with situations
    D. all of the above

21. Manifestations of agitation and restlessness are wide-ranging in both form and severity, including all of the following EXCEPT

    A. long attention span
    B. constantly moving hands, e.g., picking at clothing, dressing and undressing, hand wringing, and twisting paper
    C. an inability to sit still, even for meals
    D. prowling aimlessly about neighborhood

22. Evidences that the everyday living of these agitated and restless elderly persons is not being managed effectively include

    A. exhaustion from lack of sleep or rest
    B. weight loss from burning more calories than they take time to eat
    C. being abused, assaulted, or robbed
    D. all of the above

23. Of the following, which is NOT a goal of nursing treatment plans for restless and agitated persons?

    A. Maintaining nutrition and elimination
    B. Arranging for adequate sleep and rest
    C. Providing a safe, completely isolated environment
    D. Providing for a more comfortable lifestyle

24. Older persons who are MORE likely to manage their current daily living by engaging in aggressive, hostile, and combative behavior are usually

    A. experiencing hearing or vision losses
    B. sharing living space with a person who has similar sensory deficits
    C. frustrated with self at being unable to do what was formerly possible
    D. all of the above

25. Factors that predict the likelihood of hostile, combative behavior continuing as an element in daily living include all of the following EXCEPT

    A. previous pattern of episodes of this behavior
    B. evidence of such behavior in the family
    C. nature of the events that triggers the behavior and the likelihood that such events will recur
    D. the nature of reinforcement the behavior has received

KEY (CORRECT ANSWERS)

1.	D	11.	B
2.	B	12.	A
3.	A	13.	D
4.	D	14.	B
5.	C	15.	C
6.	D	16.	B
7.	A	17.	C
8.	D	18.	C
9.	B	19.	B
10.	D	20.	A

21. A
22. D
23. C
24. D
25. B

EXAMINATION SECTION
TEST 1

DIRECTIONS: Each question or incomplete statement is followed by several suggested answers or completions. Select the one that BEST answers the question or completes the statement. *PRINT THE LETTER OF THE CORRECT ANSWER IN THE SPACE AT THE RIGHT.*

1. The general principles a nurse should follow to aid in the prevention of destructive outbursts in elderly people include all of the following EXCEPT

    A. discussing with the patient factors that stimulate hostility or aggression and giving argument to resolve conflicts
    B. never threatening, scolding, punishing, or shaming the person
    C. redirecting troublesome behavior into constructive channels
    D. quietly giving short, simple, direct responses to prevent additional confusion

    1.____

2. Depression may alter patterns and styles of daily living. Depression generally does NOT cause

    A. erratic sleeping patterns varying from insomnia to excessive sleep
    B. a decrease in somatic complaints
    C. withdrawal from friends, family, and environment
    D. talk of suicide or suicide attempts

    2.____

3. Short-term memory has a small capacity and is useful for almost instantaneous recollection.
Factors that increase the risk of short-term memory loss include all of the following EXCEPT

    A. shortened sensory overload
    B. CNS or circulatory deficits
    C. poor nutritional status
    D. hearing losses and visual deficits

    3.____

4. Early in short-term memory loss, older persons may engage in behavior to cover for memory losses.
Later manifestations of more severe memory loss in elderly persons include

    A. failure to recognize when clothing is soiled, forgetting to bathe, wearing clothing longer than has been normal for them
    B. forgetting to prepare food or to eat
    C. forgetting to take medications according to regimen
    D. all of the above

    4.____

5. Some older people create difficulties in daily living, not only for themselves, but also for all those around them.
All of the following are guidelines that caregivers and family members can use in dealing with these negative individuals EXCEPT:

    A. Set realistic goals with the person and be constructive
    B. Do not get the person involved in doing an activity

    5.____

33

C. Accept the deprecating, complaining behavior, but continue to recognize positive contributions and outcomes, even as the person negates them
D. Agree on an approach in which all staff members and family members will behave consistently in responding to specified behavior

6. Nursing management of loneliness should never take a shotgun approach. Any intervention needs to be based on a validated diagnosis of the presence of loneliness plus the individual's

   A. times of greatest discomfort or risk
   B. goals for human intimacy
   C. current coping behavior
   D. all of the above

7. Diagnostic criteria for alcohol abuse does NOT include

   A. alcohol needed when an extra amount of work, besides the normal daily activities, needs to be done
   B. inability to cut down or stop drinking
   C. amnestic periods for events occurring while intoxicated
   D. continuation of drinking despite a serious physical disorder that the individual knows is exacerbated by alcohol use

8. Alcoholism in the elderly contributes to skeletal defects by causing

   A. osteoporosis
   B. risk of fractures through trauma
   C. both of the above
   D. none of the above

9. There are several conditions occurring in the central nervous system that are closely associated with long-term alcohol abuse.
   These include all of the following EXCEPT

   A. cerebellar degeneration   B. amyotropic lateral sclerosis
   C. central pontine myelinolysis   D. pallegra

10. Regarding common drugs and their interactions with alcohol, the use of _____ increases the risk of hypotension.

    A. nitroglycerin   B. monoamine oxidase
    C. both of the above   D. none of the above

11. Cancer of the colon and rectum are found most often in the elderly.
    Changes in bowel habits and character of stool require the older person to be a good observer and historian, as well as one who can remember other coexisting factors, including

    A. amount of water and other fluids taken during the time period
    B. types of food eaten, for example, fatty foods, no protein, high proteins, or only carbohydrates
    C. changes in activities and exercise patterns
    D. all of the above

12. In cancer detection approaches in the elderly, _____ may be used to detect cancer of the breast.

    A. breast self-examination
    B. mammography
    C. both of the above
    D. none of the above

13. Some elderly persons temporarily or permanently lose their full ability to masticate, to move the food bolus to the posterior pharynx, or to swallow the bolus to a patent esophagus, stomach, and intestinal tract. Treatment factors that cause such dysfunctions include all of the following EXCEPT

    A. untreated malignancy or metastatic disease of the oropharynx, larynx, esophagus, or gastrointestinal tract
    B. implanted dentures
    C. trismus as a sequel to radiation, edema, or infection
    D. implanted iridium needles in the tongue or floor of the mouth

14. After exposure to an accumulation of 5,000 rads or a total body exposure of 1,000 rads, changes in composition and consistency of saliva occur and it becomes ropy and tenacious.
    These changes provide a positive environment for infection by

    A. candidiasis
    B. herpes simplex infection
    C. both of the above
    D. none of the above

15. Of the following people, those at LEAST risk for managing their daily nutrition in the face of pain and dysphagia are those who

    A. were previously malnourished as a consequence of alcoholism
    B. are taking excessive analgesics
    C. maintained poor oral hygiene prior to, during, and after delivery
    D. have a solitary lifestyle with few personal support symptoms

16. Nursing strategies useful in managing difficulties in eating include all of the following EXCEPT

    A. no analgesia prior to eating
    B. oral hygiene to remove debris, plaque, and tenacious secretions
    C. use of deglutition spoon or modified syringe for liquid diets
    D. considering the option of enteral feeding or hyperalimentation

17. A nurse evaluating the patients response to living each day with the inability to eat should collect data on the status of

    A. oropharyngeal tissues
    B. gingiva and the ability to wear dentures or partials
    C. eating and swallowing skills
    D. all of the above

18. In the over-70 age group, even uncomplicated and successful surgery for cancer results in prolonged low energy levels for almost a year. Certain factors can be predicted to produce periods of low energy.
    Of the following, the factor that does NOT produce low energy is

    A. presence of other decompensating chronic disease
    B. early stages of metastatic disease
    C. neoplastic diseases in which fatigue is an initial and ongoing feature
    D. insomnia or sleep interruptions

19. Emotional components that contribute to low energy in elderly persons with cancer include all of the following EXCEPT

    A. feeling abandoned by the family or health care providers
    B. pleasant interpersonal relationships
    C. tasks demanding prolonged activity or concentration
    D. social events

20. All of the following conditions or situations decrease the ability to tolerate pain EXCEPT

    A. presence of gastrointestinal symptoms, for example, nausea, vomiting, diarrhea, constipation, impactions
    B. constant weight loss or cachexia
    C. excessive sleep
    D. emotional upset, such as anxiety, depression, fear, and anger

21. The factors in cancer and its treatment that increase vulnerability to infection do NOT include

    A. breakdown of skin and mucosal barriers due to tumor mass or treatment modalities
    B. neutropenia and malnutrition
    C. increased phagocytic function of leukocytes
    D. impaired antibody production

22. The best treatment for infection in older persons with cancer is prevention. The nursing regimen for prevention includes involving the patient and family in all of the following EXCEPT

    A. learning safe handwashing and oral hygiene techniques and patterns
    B. starting with prophylactic antibiotics
    C. learning safe laundry techniques and the importance of changing particular items of clothing and bedding regularly
    D. learning how to clean humidifiers and respirators, oxygen tubing, or other treatment instruments used in daily care

23. The older person with cancer experiences multiple separations in daily living with the disease and its treatment. Persons well-equipped to handle the separations associated with cancer are those who

    A. feel helpless or hopeless
    B. live alone or have diminishing contact with family and friends, particularly age-mates or favorite people
    C. suffer severe pain or intractable nausea and vomiting
    D. none of the above

24. Drug treatment can increase the risk of congestive cardiac failure. Inadequate or over- zealous drug therapy can precipitate congestive heart failure.
Drugs with this potential to affect congestive cardiac and heart failure do NOT include

   A. beta-adrenergic blockers
   B. calcium channel blockers
   C. digoxin
   D. alcohol

24.____

25. The most severe complication associated with congestive heart failure is the development of other end-stage organ disease as a result of chronic perfusion reduction.
The goals of treatment that nurses should keep in mind include all of the following EXCEPT

   A. increase cardiac preload
   B. reduce sodium and water retention
   C. improve contractility of heart
   D. reduce cardiac workload

25.____

KEY (CORRECT ANSWERS)

1. A		11. D	
2. B		12. C	
3. A		13. B	
4. D		14. C	
5. B		15. B	
6. D		16. A	
7. A		17. D	
8. C		18. B	
9. B		19. B	
10. A		20. C	

21. C
22. B
23. D
24. B
25. A

TEST 2

DIRECTIONS: Each question or incomplete statement is followed by several suggested answers or completions. Select the one that BEST answers the question or completes the statement. *PRINT THE LETTER OF THE CORRECT ANSWER IN THE SPACE AT THE RIGHT.*

1. In elderly patients with CHF, methods used to decrease cardiac workload include

   A. vasodilators to reduce peripheral vascular resistance
   B. weight reduction
   C. both of the above
   D. none of the above

2. Digitalis, a cardiac glycoside, is the standard treatment for increasing the force and velocity of each contraction. Factors that influence the individuals sensitivity to digitalis include

   A. fluid and electrolyte balance, particularly sodium and potassium
   B. concomitant drug therapies, for example, anti-arrhythmics, catecholamines
   C. altered thyroid or renal function
   D. all of the above

3. While all older persons are at risk for arterial occlusive disease, there are some factors that increase the risk, including all of the following EXCEPT

   A. being a female
   B. having diabetes mellitus
   C. being a smoker
   D. having a history of coronary artery disease or cerebrovascular disease

4. Complications associated with ischemic heart disease in the elderly do NOT include

   A. cardiac failure
   B. thyrotoxicosis
   C. cardiac rupture
   D. pulmonary embolism

5. The nursing goals of treatment for older persons with ischemic heart disease include

   A. increasing myocardial oxygen supply
   B. reducing myocardial oxygen demand
   C. both of the above
   D. none of the above

6. Arterial occlusive disease can range from inconvenience to a severely debilitating disease with serious ischemia and infarction of tissues in the lower extremities. Treatment of arterial occlusive disease in the elderly includes all of the following EXCEPT

   A. slowing the progression of the disease
   B. increasing collateral circulation
   C. increasing the cardiac afterload
   D. maintaining skin integrity

7. Congestive cardiac failure and other cardiac pathology commonly results in shortness of breath and reduced strength and endurance.
NOT included among the complications in daily living that may occur if it is not managed effectively is

   A. discouragement and depression leading to slow suicide by misuse of medications, sodium consumption, not eating, and self-neglect
   B. excessive sleepiness
   C. malnutrition secondary to anorexia and the inability to shop for or prepare food
   D. use of high sodium convenience food

7.____

8. Chronic congestive heart failure and its treatment affect appetite and digestion in several ways.
Factors that increase the problems experienced with food and eating include all of the following EXCEPT

   A. hepatic engorgement and enlarged heart
   B. dyspnea and decreased energy for eating
   C. splenic infarction
   D. persistent electrolyte imbalance

8.____

9. Managing eating with the side effects of congestive heart failure can be predicted on the basis of the persons

   A. capacity and eternal resources for purchasing and preparing meals
   B. understanding and acceptance of diet as an important factor in health status and relative well-being
   C. desire to live
   D. all of the above

9.____

10. Failure to incorporate appropriate eating into daily living with congestive heart failure can produce a downward spiral in which not eating results in even lessened hunger and leads to all of the following EXCEPT

    A. growing weakness
    B. increasing hepatic and splenic failure
    C. infection
    D. growing cardiac and serum chemistry

10.____

11. Prognostic variables on managing daily living with leg pain and intermittent claudication include

    A. rate of progression of the disease and symptoms present
    B. older persons motivation to begin and continue a prescribed exercise program
    C. previous capacity to make adjustments in daily living
    D. all of the above

11.____

12. Inability to manage daily living effectively because of leg pain and intermittent claudication in an elderly patient with congestive heart failure will most likely NOT result in

    A. social isolation because of inability to get out
    B. ulceration, gangrene, failure to manage acute emergencies, and resultant amputation or death

12.____

C. an angry feeling towards the staff with homicidal ideation
D. malnutrition

13. The nursing regimen in a patient of congestive heart failure with leg pain and intermittent claudication includes planning with the older person or primary care-givers on specific management of daily living as it relates to all of the following EXCEPT

    A. keeping the leg acutely flexed at the hips to enhance circulation
    B. externally supporting leg tissues
    C. planning activities ahead to reduce unnecessary walking in daily chores
    D. planning for alternatives

14. EFFECTIVE management of daily living with symptomatic peripheral vascular disease can be evaluated in terms of the

    A. amount of walking that can be done prior to onset of pain
    B. maintenance of personal care and nutritional status
    C. status of personal feeling of well-being
    D. all of the above

15. In the elderly, leg ulcers heal very slowly, if at all. Deterrents to managing daily living effectively with leg ulcers and their treatment do NOT include

    A. extensive deep, bilateral or infected ulcers
    B. hyperesthesia in legs
    C. lack of assistance in wound care, chores, and transportation
    D. lack of money for supplies and medications

16. Nursing interventions in the management of daily living with leg ulcers include all of the following EXCEPT

    A. teaching dressing, soaking, and wound cleaning techniques as needed
    B. trying to adopt a sitting posture most of the time, keeping the legs down
    C. as debridement is very painful, analgesics can be taken before an office visit
    D. helping the person deal with the reality of the slowness of the healing of ulcers, despite the best of care

17. Certain older persons are at greater risk of managing daily living by not dealing with the signs and symptoms of transient ischemic attacks.
    Of the following, the only people NOT at increased risk are those who

    A. are continuously talking about these minor complaints to the doctor
    B. attribute the signs and symptoms of transient ischemic attacks to aging
    C. have an unclear mental status
    D. are loners with few close associates to recognize changes in their physical and mental states

18. Good prognosis for the effective management of daily living in an elderly patient with transient ischemic attacks includes

    A. being totally preoccupied with the threat and risks of transient ischemic attacks
    B. having a backup support system
    C. having poor skills or an inadequate plan for reporting the symptoms experienced
    D. all of the above

19. Nursing interventions in an elderly patient with transient ischemic attacks addresses several areas of daily living. These interventions include all of the following activities EXCEPT

    A. encouraging or assisting the older person to find a physician or clinician in whom he has confidence
    B. locating the telephone at bedside
    C. encouraging the patient for sudden rapid changes of position and movement
    D. improving the safety of the environment in the home

20. Of the following individuals, those NOT at higher risk for not being able to manage daily living with altered speech and comprehension include those who

    A. live with people or in a community where there is little understanding of the dynamics of pathology
    B. were very non-verbal prior to their stroke
    C. go out in a community where their condition is not recognized or understood
    D. lack a consistent companion

21. A person who recovers from a major stroke faces a long rehabilitation period. Rationale for use of the evaluation flow sheet includes the desire to

    A. assess improvements of functions
    B. enhance self-esteem and body image
    C. recall how much progress has been made since the onset of disability
    D. all of the above

22. The cornerstone of treatment of diabetes mellitus is diet.
    The goal of diet treatment includes all of the following EXCEPT

    A. achievement and maintenance of ideal body weight
    B. taking concentrated carbohydrates
    C. avoidance of wide swings of blood pressure
    D. normal blood fats

23. Factors responsible for symptomatology of hypoglycemia in an elderly patient with diabetes mellitus include

    A. decreased glucose available to brain
    B. epinephrine release with a sympathetic nervous system response
    C. both of the above
    D. none of the above

24. Guidelines for the diabetic patient or for people responsible for the diabetic patient include:

    A. Inspecting feet daily for blisters, breaks, calluses, and bruises
    B. Washing with mild soap and then soaking in water for 15 minutes
    C. Avoiding stockings with holes or mended places
    D. All of the above

25. Helping an older person cope with diabetes is a complex situation.
A realistic look at the elderly person seems to justify adjustment of all of the following goals EXCEPT

    A. attainment and maintenance of ideal body weight
    B. presence of hypoglycemia
    C. absence of acidosis and ketonuria
    D. absence of atrophy or scarring of hypertrophy at injection sites

KEY (CORRECT ANSWERS)

1.	C	11.	D
2.	D	12.	C
3.	A	13.	A
4.	B	14.	D
5.	C	15.	B
6.	C	16.	B
7.	B	17.	A
8.	C	18.	B
9.	D	19.	C
10.	B	20.	B

21. D
22. B
23. C
24. D
25. B

EXAMINATION SECTION
TEST 1

DIRECTIONS: Each question or incomplete statement is followed by several suggested answers or completions. Select the one that BEST answers the question or completes the statement. *PRINT THE LETTER OF THE CORRECT ANSWER IN THE SPACE AT THE RIGHT.*

1. The Framingham study set a commonly accepted estimation of obesity, which was body weight of _____ % or more above ideal conditions. 1.____

    A. 5   B. 10   C. 20   D. 40

2. The mortality curve for body mass is BEST described as 2.____

    A. increased mortality at the high end
    B. increased mortality at the low end
    C. increased mortality at high and low ends
    D. low mortality at the low end, gradually increasing with increasing body mass

3. Obesity is the leading predisposing cause for 3.____
    I. adult onset diabetes
    II. breast cancer
    III. hypertension
    The CORRECT answer is:

    A. I, II   B. I, III   C. II, III   D. I, II, III

4. A vitamin deficiency that can cause nonspecific dementia or gait and balance problems in the absence of specific hematologic or spinal cord traits is 4.____

    A. vitamin A   B. vitamin B_{12}
    C. vitamin D   D. folate

5. The vitamin that is pivotal in bone health is 5.____

    A. vitamin A   B. vitamin B_{12}
    C. vitamin D   D. folate

6. _____ is primarily a deficiency of protein. 6.____

    A. Kwashiorkor   B. Marasmus
    C. Osteomalacia   D. Osteopenia

7. Which of the following tubes would be used for short-term feedings? 7.____

    A. Gastrostomy   B. Gastrotomy
    C. Jejunostomy   D. Nasoenteric

8. A common complication of feeding tubes is 8.____

    A. aspiration pneumonia   B. dehydration
    C. failure to thrive   D. GI malabsorption

9. Which of the following would be considered an unreliable sign of dehydration in the elderly?

   A. Poor skin turgor
   B. Postural hypotension
   C. Tachycardia
   D. Weight loss

10. Which of the following would be considered a state of overhydration?

    A. Congestive heart failure
    B. Diarrhea
    C. Increased diuresis
    D. Weight gain

11. The elderly use prescription drugs _____ as the general population.

    A. in the same proportion
    B. twice as much
    C. four times as much
    D. ten times as much

12. Which of the following medications are known to cause confusion in the elderly?
    I. Diphenhydramine
    II. Beta blockers
    III. Cimetadine

    The CORRECT answer is:

    A. I, II
    B. I, III
    C. II, III
    D. I, II, III

13. The term commonly used to describe the use of many medications in the elderly is

    A. drug abuse
    B. metapharmacy
    C. pharmacokinetics
    D. polypharmacy

14. The absorption, distribution, metabolism, and excretion of medications is known as

    A. drug action
    B. metapharmacy
    C. pharmacokinetics
    D. polypharmacy

15. Creatinine clearance from age 25 to 85

    A. *increases* slightly (approximately 10%)
    B. *increases* greatly (approximately 50%)
    C. *decreases* slightly (approximately 10%)
    D. *decreases* greatly (approximately 50%)

16. Blood flow through the liver _____ from age 25 to 85.

    A. *increases* slightly (approximately 10%)
    B. *increases* greatly (approximately 50%)
    C. *decreases* slightly (approximately 10%)
    D. *decreases* greatly (approximately 50%)

17. The way in which the body responds to drugs is known as

    A. metapharmacy
    B. pharmacodynamics
    C. pharmacokinetics
    D. polypharmacy

18. The anticholinergic effects of medications may cause 18.____

    A. confusion
    B. decreased kidney function
    C. decreased liver function
    D. tachycardia

19. Which ethnic group has shown the largest increase in life expectancy over the last 50 years? 19.____

    A. African-Americans B. Caucasians
    C. Hispanics   D. Japanese

20. For a pressure sore, erythema would be classified as stage 20.____

    A. I   B. II   C. III   D. IV

21. The ADL (activity of daily living) that the FEWEST number of elderly need assistance with is 21.____

    A. bathing   B. dressing   C. eating   D. walking

22. About what percentage of elderly living in the community have at least some problems with incontinence? 22.____

    A. 1   B. 3   C. 10   D. 33

23. Which of the following statements is true regarding blood pressure and aging? 23.____

    A. Both systolic and diastolic pressures tend to increase with age.
    B. Both systolic and diastolic pressures tend to decrease with age.
    C. Diastolic pressure increases up to about 65, then decreases, whereas systolic continues to increase with age.
    D. Systolic pressure increases up to about 65, then decreases, whereas diastolic continues to increase with age.

24. Which of the following is a CORRECT statement? 24.____
    _____ are able to perform instrumental activities of daily living.

    A. Most older adults (more than 85%)
    B. Most older adults (just over 50%)
    C. A minority of older adults (under 50%)
    D. A minority of older adults (under 25%)

25. Which of the following is a CORRECT statement? 25.____

    A. Later life is marked by an increase in hypochondriasis.
    B. Later life is not marked by an increase in hypochondriasis.
    C. Older adults are more likely to report physical symptoms of disease than younger people.
    D. There are major differences in the coping strategies used by older people as compared to younger people.

KEY (CORRECT ANSWERS)

1. C
2. C
3. B
4. B
5. C

6. A
7. D
8. A
9. A
10. A

11. B
12. D
13. D
14. C
15. D

16. D
17. B
18. A
19. A
20. A

21. C
22. D
23. C
24. A
25. B

TEST 2

DIRECTIONS: Each question or incomplete statement is followed by several suggested answers or completions. Select the one that BEST answers the question or completes the statement. *PRINT THE LETTER OF THE CORRECT ANSWER IN THE SPACE AT THE RIGHT.*

1. Which legal decision held that artificial means of feeding and hydration were medical treatments?

    A. Darling
    B. Cruzan
    C. Kervorkian
    D. Older Americans Act

2. The most common form of deep heat used in physical medicine is

    A. hot packs
    B. hydrotherapy
    C. paraffin baths
    D. ultrasound

3. Which of the following is the leading cause of death from unintentional injury for individuals over the age of 75%

    A. Automobile crashes
    B. Electrocution
    C. Exposure (cold)
    D. Falls

4. Which of the following visual diseases has the highest incidence in the elderly?

    A. Cataracts
    B. Diabetic retinopathy
    C. Glaucoma
    D. Macular degeneration

5. Which of the following have been implicated in urinary incontinence?
    I. Delirium
    II. Reduced mobility
    III. Stool impaction
    The CORRECT answer is:

    A. I, II
    B. I, III
    C. II, III
    D. I, II, III

6. Which of the following is also known as stress incontinence?

    A. Detrusor overactivity
    B. Detrusor underactivity
    C. Outlet incompetence
    D. Outlet obstruction

7. Which of the following is most common in men?

    A. Detrusor overactivity
    B. Detrusor underactivity
    C. Outlet incompetence
    D. Outlet obstruction

8. Which of the following occurs when inhibition of bladder contractions is lost and the bladder contracts precipi-tantly, leading to urinary leakage?

    A. Detrusor overactivity
    B. Detrusor underactivity
    C. Outlet incompetence
    D. Outlet obstruction

9. All pressure ulcers greater than stage _____ will be colonized with bacteria

    A. I
    B. II
    C. III
    D. IV

10. The common ocular complaint of the elderly, being less able to focus clearly at normal distances, is called

    A. anopthalmia
    B. diplopia
    C. presbycusis
    D. presbyopia

11. The most common class of drugs given for treatment of depression are the

    A. atypical antidepressants
    B. monoamine oxidase inhibitors
    C. stimulants
    D. tricyclic antidepressants

12. Which of the following is a type of frontal lobe degeneration? _____ disease.

    A. Alzheimer's
    B. Parkinson's
    C. Pick's
    D. Wilson's

13. The most common cause of cerebral infarction is

    A. atherosclerotic vascular disease
    B. cardiac disease
    C. elevated hematocrit
    D. polycythemia vera

14. Which of the following are recommended as prophylactic therapy for stroke when anticoagulants such as Coumadin cannot be used?

    A. Altepase
    B. Aspirin
    C. Streptokinase
    D. Surgery

15. Which type of stroke carries the greatest risk of mortality and morbidity? _____ hemorrhage.

    A. Intracerebellar
    B. Primary intracerebral
    C. Secondary intracerebral
    D. Subarachnoid

16. Most incidences of Parkinson's disease fall into which one of the following categories?

    A. Atherosclerotic
    B. Drug-induced
    C. Idiopathic
    D. Postencephalitic

17. The Framingham study showed that the leading cause of congestive heart failure in all ages, but especially in the elderly, was

    A. cardiomyopathy
    B. hypertension
    C. infective heart disease
    D. valvular heart disease

18. Which of the following heart diseases would be considered somewhat specific to the elderly population?

    A. Cardiomyopathy
    B. Calcific heart disease
    C. Hypertensive heart disease
    D. Valvular heart disease

19. Which of the following is NOT true?

    A. Males have an increased risk for Colles' fractures.
    B. Females have an increased risk for hip fractures.
    C. About 1/3 of women over age 65 will have one or more vertebral compression fractures.
    D. About 8 percent of long-term care patients have had a diagnosis of hip fracture.

20. Which of the following is NOT true?

    A. Overweight females have a lessened risk of developing osteoporosis.
    B. Blacks tend to have less incidence of osteoporosis than whites.
    C. Tobacco has a deleterious effect on bone mass density.
    D. Increased calcium intake does not appear to reduce the risk of hip fracture.

21. Which of the following is the LEAST useful in making a diagnosis of osteoporosis?

    A. Computed tomography
    B. Dual photon absorptiometry
    C. Radiography
    D. Single photon absorptiometry

22. Which of the following conditions provides the highest level of morbidity (in terms of number of people affected) in the elderly population?

    A. Arthritis
    B. Diabetes
    C. Cataracts
    D. Heart conditions

23. Heel spurs are also known as

    A. clavi
    B. hallux valgus
    C. plantar keratosis
    D. plantar fascitis

24. *Corns* are also known as

    A. clavi
    B. hallux valgus
    C. plantar keratosis
    D. plantar fascitis

25. Which of the following very commonly affects the first metatarsophalangeal joint?
    I. Gout
    II. Osteoarthritis
    III. Rheumatoid arthritis
    The CORRECT answer is:

    A. I, II
    B. I, III
    C. II, III
    D. I, II, III

KEY (CORRECT ANSWERS)

1. B
2. D
3. D
4. A
5. D

6. C
7. D
8. A
9. B
10. D

11. D
12. C
13. A
14. B
15. B

16. C
17. B
18. B
19. A
20. D

21. C
22. A
23. D
24. A
25. A

———

EXAMINATION SECTION
TEST 1

DIRECTIONS: Each question or incomplete statement is followed by several suggested answers or completions. Select the one that BEST answers the question or completes the statement. *PRINT THE LETTER OF THE CORRECT ANSWER IN THE SPACE AT THE RIGHT.*

1. Which of the following is NOT universal among cultures? 1.____

   A. The aged are always a minority.
   B. Females always outnumber males.
   C. All older people are treated differently because they are old.
   D. Social mores mandate that older people must be segregated from the younger population.

2. Which of the following characterizes Erik Erikson's *crisis* central to old age? 2.____

   A. Intimacy versus isolation
   B. Ego identity versus identity confusion
   C. Generativity versus stagnation
   D. Integrity versus despair

3. Which theorist/researcher first examined the life review in relation to old age? 3.____

   A. Butler   B. Erikson   C. Freud   D. Levinson

4. The danger in stage theories of aging (as well as stage theories such as Kuebler-Ross's of death and dying) is to view them as _____ rather than _____. 4.____

   A. accurate; false
   B. false; accurate
   C. descriptive; prescriptive
   D. prescriptive; descriptive

5. Which theory holds that decreased involvement of elders in society is beneficial? 5.____

   A. Activity   B. Disengagement
   C. Learned helplessness D. Life satisfaction

6. Which theory has been criticized for treating the elderly as if they were *already dead*? 6.____

   A. Activity   B. Disengagement
   C. Learned helplessness D. Life satisfaction

7. Which theory can be critiqued for assuming that individuals perhaps have more control over their lives than they really do? 7.____

   A. Activity   B. Disengagement
   C. Learned helplessness D. Life satisfaction

8. Which classification of death assumes that systems will no longer be able to regenerate themselves?

   A. Biological
   B. Brain
   C. Cerebral
   D. Clinical

9. Which one of the following dementias has been implicated as genetic in origin?

   A. Creutzfeld-Jakob disease
   B. Huntington's chorea
   C. Multi-infract dementia
   D. Normal pressure hydrocephalus

10. Korsakoff's syndrome is a dementia caused by

    A. infection
    B. intracranial mass
    C. toxicity
    D. vascular deficits

11. Depression can mimic dementia in a type of pseudodementia. Which of the following signs would characterize pseudo-dementia?
    I. Rapid onset/duration
    II. Vague complaints of cognitive loss
    III. Attention and concentration remain relatively intact
    The CORRECT answer is:

    A. I, II
    B. I, III
    C. II, III
    D. I, II, III

12. The development of a therapeutic community is used in _____ therapy.

    A. environmental
    B. milieu
    C. reality
    D. remotivation

13. The growing inability to suppress irrelevant stimuli with age is known as the _____ theory.

    A. central processing
    B. neural noise
    C. perceptual noise
    D. selective attention

14. Assuming that the healthy portion of an individual's personality can be activated via restructuring the environment is used in _____ therapy.

    A. environmental
    B. milieu
    C. reality
    D. remotivation

15. Which of the following is NOT true regarding tooth loss in the elderly? Tooth loss is

    A. correlated with lower incomes
    B. usually a result of lack of proper dental care
    C. inevitable in the elderly
    D. often due to pyorrhea

16. In the large intestine, cancer occurs most frequently in the

    A. left colon
    B. rectum
    C. right colon
    D. sigmoid colon

17. Which of the following is true regarding the presentation of osteomalacia (as opposed to osteoporosis)?

    A. Muscle weakness is rarely present.
    B. Axial bones are more commonly affected.
    C. No presence of skeletal pain.
    D. Abnormal values for serum calcium

18. In 1972, the act that generated a national program for one nutritionally planned hot meal a day, 5 days a week, for people age 60 and over was the

    A. Comprehensive Services Amendment to the Older Americans Act
    B. Commodities Distribution Program
    C. Food Stamp Act
    D. Home Health Services Act

19. Which of the following are correct regarding urinalysis in the elderly?
    I. Asymptomatic pyuria is uncommon and should be furtherevaluated.
    II. Asymptomatic bacteriuria is common.
    III. Hematuria is uncommon and should be further evaluated.

    The CORRECT answer is:

    A. I, II   B. I, III   C. II, III   D. I, II, III

20. Which one of the following laboratory tests should remain unchanged in the elderly (i.e., aging changes do not occur in its parameters)?

    A. Blood urea nitrogen
    B. Glucose tolerance
    C. Prostate specific antigen
    D. Sedimentation rate

21. Which of the following are true?
    I. Medicare Part A is hospital services insurance.
    II. Medicare Part B is medical services insurance.
    III. Fees are charged for both Parts A and B.

    The CORRECT answer is:

    A. I, II   B. I, III   C. II, III   D. I, II, III

22. Title XX of the Social Security Act covers

    A. day care
    B. hospital services
    C. legal services and counseling
    D. medical services

23. Meals on Wheels programs are generally funded through

    A. Title III   B. Title XX   C. Medicare   D. Medicaid

24. Which of the following programs is capped at an annual appropriation level, requiring matching funds in cash or in kind?

    A. Title III   B. Title XX   C. Medicare   D. Medicaid

25. Which of the following is NOT true?

    A. Total spending for nursing home care for those age 65 and above is about evenly divided between public and private expenditures.
    B. Acute care is more often paid by third-party payers than long-term care.
    C. The major public funding sources for long-term care are Title XX and the Older Americans Act.
    D. Medicare does no funding of long-term care.

KEY (CORRECT ANSWERS)

1.	D		11.	B
2.	D		12.	B
3.	A		13.	C
4.	D		14.	D
5.	B		15.	C
6.	B		16.	B
7.	A		17.	D
8.	A		18.	A
9.	B		19.	C
10.	C		20.	A

21. A
22. A
23. A
24. A
25. D

TEST 2

DIRECTIONS: Each question or incomplete statement is followed by several suggested answers or completions. Select the one that BEST answers the question or completes the statement. *PRINT THE LETTER OF THE CORRECT ANSWER IN THE SPACE AT THE RIGHT.*

1. Which of the following best describes *compression of morbidity*? 1.____

    A. The postponement of death into advanced old age
    B. The postponement of disability and illness into advanced old age
    C. A reduction in death rates
    D. A reduction in disability and illness

2. The MAJOR funding source for adult day care is 2.____

    A. Medicaid B. Medicare
    C. Philanthropy D. Title III

3. Which of the following is an INSTRUMENTAL activity of daily living (IADL)? 3.____

    A. Bathing B. Feeding C. Shopping D. Toileting

4. Which of the following is a Social Security Administration classification for relatives of elderly individuals unable to manage their financial affairs due to physical or mental impairment? 4.____

    A. Guardianship B. Legal guardianship
    C. Power of attorney D. Payee status

5. Which of the following is true? 5.____

    A. Fingernails are more prone to thicken with age than toenails.
    B. Most nail changes due to aging are due to diminished vascular supply.
    C. Nutritional status has not been implicated in age-related changes of the nails.
    D. Aging nails become less brittle and hard.

6. The primary etiology for pathological changes in aging skin is exposure to 6.____

    A. allergens B. climate
    C. industrial contaminants D. sunlight

7. Shingles is also known as herpes 7.____

    A. melanogaster B. simplex
    C. varicellae D. zoster

8. A condition of older age in which there is excessive resorption and deposition of bone is 8.____

    A. osteoarthritis B. osteomalacia
    C. osteoporosis D. Paget's disease

9. In rheumatoid arthritis, morning stiffness lasts _____ with pain most severe in the _____. 9.____

    A. 10 to 30 minutes; morning
    B. 1 hour or longer; morning

55

C. 10 to 30 minutes; evening
D. 1 hour or longer; evening

10. A man over the age of 62 would probably be considered anemic if his hemoglobin was less than _____ g/100.

    A. 13   B. 15   C. 17   D. 19

11. The theory that holds that abused children may abuse their parents in later life is the _____ theory.

    A. dependency
    B. psychopathology of the abuser
    C. social learning (transgenerational)
    D. stressed caregiver

12. In elder abuse, the abuser is most likely a

    A. child caregiver   B. nurse or nurse's aid
    C. spouse   D. stranger

13. Which of the following is sometimes (unjustly) overlooked in assessments of the elderly and may explain behaviors such as inattention to bathing and malnutrition despite adequate foodstuffs?

    A. Kinesthesia   B. Olfaction
    C. Sensory overload   D. Touch

14. Which of the following is true regarding weight loss and gain in the elderly?

    A. Normal weight men tend to gain weight after age 70.
    B. Normal weight women tend to lose weight after age 70.
    C. Overweight individuals of both sexes tend to lose weight with age.
    D. Subcutaneous fat distribution does not change with age.

15. Which of the following is true regarding body composition changes with age?

    A. The specific gravity of the body increases with age.
    B. Fat concentration decreases by about 16 percent from age 25 to 75.
    C. Water content increases by about 8 percent from age 25 to 75.
    D. The extracellular component of water does not increase with age.

16. Which type of substance abuse is MOST common among the elderly?

    A. Amphetamines
    B. Alcohol
    C. Marijuana
    D. Over-the-counter and prescribed medications

17. Which of the following chronic dementias would probably be diagnosed by computed tomography or cisternography?

    A. Depression
    B. Hepatic encephalopathy
    C. Hypothyroidism
    D. Normal pressure hydrocephalus

18. Which of the following is among the most common causes of vertigo in older adults? 18.____

    A. Acoustic neuroma
    B. Labyrinthitis
    C. Meniere's disease
    D. Peripheral neuropathy

19. Which of the following statements is true? 19.____

    A. Upper respiratory infections are more common in the elderly.
    B. Lower respiratory infections are more common in the elderly.
    C. The pneumonia related mortality for individuals above 70 is 5 percent.
    D. The pneumonia related mortality for individuals above 70 is 50 percent.

20. The most common cause of iron deficiency anemia in older adults is 20.____

    A. blood loss
    B. bone marrow dysfunction
    C. hemolysis
    D. vitamin B_{12} deficiency

21. Almost all pulmonary emboli originate in the 21.____

    A. deep venous system of the legs
    B. superficial venous system of the legs
    C. heart
    D. lungs

22. The *dry mouth* that is seen in many elderly individuals is also known as 22.____

    A. asalivosis
    B. dehystomia
    C. keratosis
    D. xerostomia

23. Alternating episodes of bradycardia, normal sinus rhythm, tachycardia, and periods of long sinus pause during which the atria and ventricles are not stimulated to contract characterize 23.____

    A. atrial fibrillation
    B. digitalis toxicity
    C. heart block
    D. sick sinus syndrome

24. Which of the following conditions may be overlooked as some of its symptoms may be attributed to normal aging? 24.____

    A. Diabetes
    B. Hyperthyroidism
    C. Hypothyroidism
    D. Renal dysfunction

25. Fasting and the administration of enemas prior to some diagnostic tests can cause which of the following in the elderly? 25.____
    I. Dehydration
    II. Pseudodementia
    III. Orthostatic hypotension
    The CORRECT answer is:

    A. I, II
    B. I, III
    C. II, III
    D. I, II, III

KEY (CORRECT ANSWERS)

1. B
2. A
3. C
4. D
5. B

6. D
7. D
8. D
9. B
10. A

11. C
12. C
13. B
14. C
15. D

16. D
17. D
18. D
19. B
20. A

21. A
22. D
23. D
24. C
25. D

EXAMINATION SECTION
TEST 1

DIRECTIONS: Each question or incomplete statement is followed by several suggested answers or completions. Select the one that BEST answers the question or completes the statement. *PRINT THE LETTER OF THE CORRECT ANSWER IN THE SPACE AT THE RIGHT.*

1. Which of the following is TRUE regarding dependency ratios?

    A. The youth dependency ratio in the U.S. tends to be lower than the aged dependency ratio.
    B. Youth dependency ratios tend to fluctuate less than aged dependency ratios.
    C. Higher birth rates tend to have the greatest influence on dependency ratios.
    D. The most accurate dependency ratio is the aged dependency ratio.

    1.____

2. Which of the following is TRUE regarding sleep and aging?
    I. Older people tend to sleep more than younger people.
    II. Older people tend to have more sleep disturbances than younger people.
    III. Sleep apnea tends to increase with age.

    The CORRECT answer is:

    A. I, II   B. I, III   C. II, III   D. I, II, III

    2.____

3. What is the primary cause of loss of height with age?

    A. Arthritic changes
    B. Bone fractures
    C. Muscle tone changes
    D. Porous bones develop additional curvature

    3.____

4. Differences in decline of taste between men and women has usually been attributed to

    A. changes in the lingual muscles
    B. hormonal differences
    C. men's food biases
    D. smoking

    4.____

5. The Wechsler Adult Intelligence Scale assumes that IQ _____ from age 25 to 75.

    A. remains the same
    B. drops 10 points
    C. drops 20 points
    D. drops 40 points

    5.____

6. Which of the following is the most likely change on a Wechsler Adult Intelligence Scale (WAIS) given to an educated and intellectually active individual at ages 45 and 65: Performance would _____ and vocabulary would _____.

    A. increase; decrease
    B. increase; increase
    C. decrease; increase
    D. decrease; decrease

    6.____

7. Reaction time is most likely to increase with age if the task assigned is _____ and _____.

    A. complicated; timed
    B. complicated; untimed
    C. routine; timed
    D. routine; untimed

    7.____

8. Levinson expanded on Erikson's concept of generativity in middle adulthood by adding the relationship known as _____ in which a middle-aged adult serves as a combinati parent figure and friend to a young adult.

    A. ego integrity
    B. intimacy
    C. mentoring
    D. teaching

9. Which of the following is the only inner dimension of personality that has been documented to change with age in most studies?

    A. Dogmatism
    B. Hopefulness
    C. Introversion
    D. Risk taking

10. Personality tends to

    A. become more conservative with age
    B. become less conservative with age
    C. become more religious with age
    D. stabilize after middle age

11. Most older people would rate their overall life satisfaction as

    A. very poor
    B. poor
    C. acceptable
    D. good

12. In regards to friends and friendships among the elderly,

    A. friendships are uncommon in old age
    B. most older people have only family members as friends
    C. most older people have several friends among their peers
    D. most older people choose younger people as their friends

13. As one ages, one generally needs progressively fewer (less)

    A. calories B. minerals C. protein D. vitamins

14. About what percent of retired Americans draw Social Security?

    A. Greater than 90
    B. About 80
    C. About 60
    D. Less than 50

15. The rate of decline in functioning leading to death is called

    A. death morbidity
    B. dying curve
    C. dying trajectory
    D. terminal drop

16. A particularly large drop in intellectual skills that may indicate impending death best defines

    A. death morbidity
    B. dying curve
    C. dying trajectory
    D. terminal drop

17. The percentage of people UNDER the age of 65 who are receiving long-term care is about _____ percent.

    A. 10 B. 20 C. 40 D. 60

18. Which of the following reflects the approximate cost of a one-year stay in a long-term care facility? 18.____

    A. $5,000   B. $10,000   C. $20,000   D. $40,000

19. Retirement reduces monthly income by about _____ percent. 19.____

    A. 10   B. 20   C. 40   D. 80

20. The group of elderly people that are most likely to live in retirement communities are those with 20.____

    A. acute illnesses
    B. chronic illnesses
    C. higher socioeconomic status
    D. lower socioeconomic status

21. The individual that is most likely to have psychological problems in older age is one who 21.____

    A. makes routine visits to the physician at a young age
    B. has always had difficulty remembering
    C. has never adapted well to change
    D. is very reliant on one's spouse for support

22. Which of the following states has the greatest population of individuals over age 65? 22.____

    A. Alabama   B. Arizona   C. Florida   D. Iowa

23. The lifetime chance that someone aged 65 will ever be admitted to a long-term care facility is about _____ %. 23.____

    A. 10   B. 20   C. 40   D. 60

24. The best way to facilitate acceptance of a move among an older person is to 24.____

    A. take as little time as possible to complete the move
    B. take as much time as possible to complete the move
    C. involve the individual's family as much as possible in the move
    D. involve the individual as much as possible in the move

25. Which of the following statements is NOT true? 25.____

    A. People have to spend most of their assets to receive Medicaid.
    B. Medicare benefits for skilled nursing facility costs is limited to people who require 24 hour skilled nursing care immediately following a hospital stay.
    C. On average, Medicare will pay about 27 days of costs.
    D. Medicare will pay for personal or custodial care services such as bathing or eating.

KEY (CORRECT ANSWERS)

1. C
2. C
3. D
4. D
5. D

6. C
7. A
8. C
9. C
10. D

11. D
12. C
13. A
14. A
15. C

16. D
17. C
18. D
19. C
20. C

21. C
22. C
23. C
24. D
25. D

TEST 2

DIRECTIONS: Each question or incomplete statement is followed by several suggested answers or completions. Select the one that BEST answers the question or completes the statement. *PRINT THE LETTER OF THE CORRECT ANSWER IN THE SPACE AT THE RIGHT.*

1. Which of the following are the possibilities that a man aged 65 will spend one year or more in a nursing home in his lifetime as compared to a woman aged 65? Man _____; woman _____.

    A. 14%; 31%   B. 20%; 40%   C. 31%; 14%   D. 40%; 20%

2. A man over age 75 will most likely live

    A. alone
    B. in a nursing home
    C. with his grown children or grandchildren
    D. with his wife

3. Which of the following 70 year-olds would be the most likely to commit suicide?

    A. Black male   B. Black female
    C. Native American male D. Native American female

4. Approximately what percentage of care is provided to older relatives or friends by individuals who possess another full-time job?

    A. 5%   B. 15%   C. 25%   D. 75%

5. About what percentage of care for ADLs or IADLs is provided in the home?

    A. 10%   B. 20%   C. 40%   D. 80%

6. Which of the following would be the typical cost of a home care visit by a nurse?

    A. $15   B. $25   C. $50   D. $100

7. An orderly who abuses patients as it makes him feel powerful is doing so under _____ theory.

    A. exchange   B. stressed caregiver
    C. psychopathology   D. impairment

8. A commonality that elder abuse has with child abuse is that

    A. healthcare professionals are the individuals best able to make decisions for the patient
    B. ethnicity is not a factor in determining abuse
    C. the radiographic signs for history of abuse are similar
    D. all of the above

9. A rider attached to the Gramm-Rudman-Hollings Bill

    A. extended Social Security benefits to those 70 and older
    B. increased Medicare payments to widows

C. paid for specified nursing home care
D. none of the above

10. Which theory of elder abuse holds that it is learned?

    A. Exchange
    B. Stressed caregiver
    C. Transgenerational
    D. Impairment

11. Which theory of elder abuse holds that abuse is due to mental problems or illnesses of the abuser?

    A. Psychopathology
    B. Stressed caregiver
    C. Transgenerational
    D. Impairment

12. Fractures of the _____ are signs of elder abuse.

    A. face
    B. ribs
    C. clavicles
    D. all of the above

13. Which law tends to mitigate against the use of restraints?

    A. Older Americans Act
    B. OSHA 19-20 CFR
    C. Omnibus Reconciliation Act of 1987
    D. Thurmond Act

14. Previously undetected fractures might be seen through

    A. periosteal thickening
    B. oblique fractures of the midshafts of long bones and fingers
    C. transverse fractures of the midshafts of long bones and fingers
    D. all of the above

15. In about what percentage of individuals are dementia symptoms reversible?

    A. 0
    B. 10-20
    C. 25-35
    D. 45-55

16. Apathy and not reacting to anything going on around the individual describes

    A. emotional lability
    B. flatness of affect
    C. moondowning
    D. sundowning

17. Which of the following is an autosomal dominant disorder whose symptoms include irregular and involuntary movements of the facial muscles, intellectual decline, personality change, slurred speech, and impaired judgment?

    A. Huntington's disease
    B. Multiple sclerosis
    C. Parkinson's disease
    D. Wilson's disease

18. The most common type of vascular dementia is

    A. Binswanger's disease
    B. lacunar state
    C. multi-infarct dementia
    D. strategic infarct

19. Which of the following areas of the brain are among those most affected in Alzheimer's disease?
    I. Frontal lobes
    II. Hippocampus
    III. Temporal lobes

    The CORRECT answer is:

    A. I, II   B. I, III   C. II, III   D. I, II, III

20. Which allele has been linked with a hastened onset of Alzheimer's disease? ApoE

    A. 1   B. 2   C. 3   D. 4

21. Which of the following is a drug approved in the treatment of Alzheimer's?

    A. Acetylcholinesterase   B. Tacrine
    C. Tropicamide   D. Zidovudine

22. Which of the following is a drug that dilates the pupil of the eye and may be used to diagnose Alzheimer's?

    A. Acetylcholinesterase   B. Tacrine
    C. Tropicamide   D. Zidovudine

23. Drug abuse in the elderly is most closely associated with which of the following?

    A. Use of drugs in the younger population
    B. Ease of access to controlled substances
    C. The presence of chronic disease
    D. Decreased absorption of drugs in the body

24. In Neugarten's patterns of aging, the individual who clings to patterns established in middle age would be described as

    A. apathetic   B. constricted
    C. holding on   D. succorance-seeking

25. A recently retired man who is said to be looking forward to all the things he could not do while working is probably in the _____ phase of retirement.

    A. eclectic   B. honeymoon
    C. routinized   D. succorance-seeking

KEY (CORRECT ANSWERS)

1. A
2. D
3. C
4. B
5. D

6. D
7. A
8. C
9. D
10. C

11. A
12. D
13. C
14. D
15. B

16. B
17. A
18. C
19. D
20. D

21. C
22. C
23. C
24. C
25. B

EXAMINATION SECTION
TEST 1

DIRECTIONS: Each question or incomplete statement is followed by several suggested answers or completions. Select the one that BEST answers the question or completes the statement. *PRINT THE LETTER OF THE CORRECT ANSWER IN THE SPACE AT THE RIGHT.*

1. Left brain damage following a stroke is characterized by paralyzed _____ side and _____ deficits. 1.____

   A. right; speech-language
   B. right; spatial-perceptual
   C. left; speech-language
   D. left; spatial-perceptual

2. The MOST common adverse effect of excessive insulin is 2.____

   A. hyperglycemia   B. hypoglycemia
   C. hyperlipemia   D. hypolipemia

3. Which of the following is the most common cause of hearing loss? 3.____

   A. Excessive ear wax in the external canal
   B. Otitis media
   C. Otosclerosis
   D. Sensorineural hearing loss

4. Which of the following is NOT true? 4.____

   A. All five senses tend to decline in old age.
   B. Vital lung capacity tends to decline in old age.
   C. The majority of medical practitioners tend to give low priority to the aged.
   D. Old people tend to become more religious as they age.

5. Which of the following is NOT true? 5.____

   A. The majority of older people have incomes below the poverty line.
   B. Old people usually take longer to learn something new.
   C. Over 3/4 of the elderly are able to carry on their normal everyday activities.
   D. The majority of people over the age of 65 are not senile.

6. Which of the following is TRUE? 6.____

   A. Height does not tend to decline in old age.
   B. Older people have more acute illnesses than younger people.
   C. Older people have more chronic illnesses than younger people.
   D. Older people have more accidents in the home than younger people.

7. Which of the following is TRUE? 7.____

   A. African-American's life expectancy at age 65 is about the same as whites.
   B. Men's life expectancy at age 65 is about the same as women's.

C. Medicare pays about 75% of older people's health care costs.
D. Social Security benefits do not increase with inflation.

8. Which of the following is TRUE?

    A. Most patients with Alzheimer's act the same way.
    B. It is best not to look at older mental patients when you are talking to them.
    C. Talking to demented older patients will tend to increase their confusion.
    D. Allowing demented older patients to talk about their past may decrease feelings of depression.

9. Which of the following is NOT among the colors best seen by the elderly?

    A. Black   B. Orange   C. Red   D. Yellow

10. The percentage of the elderly with a private pension plan is approximately _____ %.

    A. 10-20
    B. 20-30
    C. 40-50
    D. greater than 80

11. An employer providing _____ is probably providing the best means for later retirement for its employees.

    A. a 401K savings plan
    B. pre-employment counseling
    C. post-employment counseling
    D. a Social Security seminar

12. Increasing frequency of angina is known as _____ angina.

    A. crescendo
    B. exertional
    C. nocturnal
    D. unstable

13. Most age-related changes in GI motility are a result of _____ changes as opposed to _____ changes.

    A. muscular; neurologic
    B. neurologic; muscular
    C. constipational; obstipational
    D. obstipational; constipational

14. The most commonly observed disease of the salivary glands in older persons is

    A. bacterial infections
    B. neoplasms
    C. sialoliths
    D. Sjoergren's syndrome

15. The best advice to a couple noting loss of sexual expression and intimacy with aging would be that this is _____ and is best handled through _____.

    A. abnormal; counseling
    B. abnormal; individual experimentation
    C. normal; counseling
    D. normal; individual experimentation

16. Workers of _____ income working for _____-sized companies are the most likely to receive pre-retirement counseling from the employer.

    A. low; small
    B. moderate; small
    C. low; moderate
    D. moderate; moderate

17. Older individuals will typically first lose the ability to hear _____ sounds.

    A. higher pitched
    B. lower pitched
    C. louder
    D. softer

18. Your local advocacy group has received a $10,000 grant to fight ageism and stereotypical views of the elderly in your community. Which method would probably bring the most dramatic and immediate results?

    A. Lectures at local elementary and high schools
    B. Brown-bag sessions at the local university
    C. Free lectures at major employers in the area
    D. Use of the mass media (newspapers, radio, television, etc.)

19. Which of the following tends to NOT change with age?

    A. Absenteeism
    B. Accidents
    C. Job satisfaction
    D. Job performance

20. A 70-year-old widower able to care for himself would probably be most likely to use the services of which of the following agencies?

    A. Adult day care
    B. Elder abuse task force
    C. Nursing home
    D. Senior citizen center

21. A group of 60 year olds with early Alzheimer's in a study carried out by a major medical center in one state finds increased levels of zinc in this group as compared to younger controls. Before identifying zinc as a common causative factor of Alzheimer's for the population at large, the researchers should investigate
    I. cohort differences
    II. environmental influences
    III. the group's metabolic rate
    The CORRECT answer is:

    A. I, II
    B. I, III
    C. II, III
    D. I, II, III

22. The most common functional disability found in older individuals is

    A. blindness
    B. hearing loss
    C. loss of mobility
    D. mental disorders

23. Which of the following terms is used to describe the post-reproductive years, primarily in women?

    A. Involution
    B. Menopause
    C. Post-reproductive maturation
    D. Senescence

24. Which of the following statements about stress and the elderly is NOT true? 24.___

    A. The ability to handle stress is affected by aging.
    B. Stress recovery in the elderly typically takes longer.
    C. Due to lessened affect, stress is never a life-threatening event in the elderly.
    D. The elderly are often able to handle stress.

25. Which of the following most closely matches a description of geriatrics? 25.___

    A. A multidisciplinary study of aging
    B. The science of aging
    C. Medical treatment of the elderly
    D. A field of aging primarily borrowing from sociology and psychology

---

KEY (CORRECT ANSWERS)

1.	A	11.	A
2.	B	12.	A
3.	A	13.	B
4.	D	14.	D
5.	A	15.	D
6.	C	16.	D
7.	A	17.	A
8.	D	18.	D
9.	A	19.	D
10.	C	20.	D

21. A
22. C
23. B
24. C
25. C

TEST 2

DIRECTIONS: Each question or incomplete statement is followed by several suggested answers or completions. Select the one that BEST answers the question or completes the statement. *PRINT THE LETTER OF THE CORRECT ANSWER IN THE SPACE AT THE RIGHT.*

1. Area Councils on Aging are a result of which legislative act?   1.____

   A. Americans with Disabilities Act
   B. Older Americans Act
   C. Omnibus Reconciliation Act of 1987
   D. Thurmond Act

2. Placing federal monies into cures for diseases that affect the majority of the elderly would most likely be seen as a _____ approach.   2.____

   A. fact-based   B. medicine-oriented
   C. utilitarian   D. veracious

3. Biological changes that diminish life and make individuals more susceptible to chronic diseases and injury best describes   3.____

   A. involution   B. menopause
   C. presbyopia   D. senescence

4. Recognizing that individuals may be able to make some choices but not others due to age-related deficits best describes   4.____

   A. ageism   B. competence
   C. gatekeeping   D. task-specific competence

5. A law that requires hospitals and nursing homes to inform clients of their rights at the time of admission is the _____ Act.   5.____

   A. National Rehabilitation
   B. Older Americans
   C. Patient Self-Determination
   D. Protection and Advocacy for Mentally Ill Individuals

6. Taking away an individual's right to choose is an example of   6.____

   A. autonomy   B. beneficence
   C. justice   D. paternalism

7. Normal disease-free movement across adulthood is called   7.____

   A. primary aging   B. secondary aging
   C. senescence   D. tertiary aging

8. Age-related changes such as puberty, menopause, and retirement are often called _____ changes.   8.____

   A. historical   B. non-normative
   C. normative   D. organismic

9. Measuring average interindividual age differences at one point across time best describes a _____ study.

    A. cross-sectional
    B. longitudinal
    C. time-lag
    D. validated

10. If a study does not look at problems faced by people in the *real world*, then it lacks _____ validity.

    A. ecological
    B. external
    C. internal
    D. non-developmental

11. Which of the following best describes Werner syndrome?
    I. A genetic premature aging inherited when both parents carry the same recessive gene
    II. Occurs primarily in infancy and lacks some age-related changes such as diabetes and cataracts
    III. Tends to occur between the ages of 15 to 20

    The CORRECT answer is:

    A. I, II
    B. I, III
    C. II, III
    D. I, II, III

12. Which of the following states has the lowest proportion of individuals above the age of 65?

    A. Alaska
    B. California
    C. New Hampshire
    D. Tennessee

13. Which of the following states has the greatest number of individuals above the age of 65?

    A. California
    B. Florida
    C. New York
    D. Texas

14. Which of the following is TRUE?

    A. Even when disease free, heart function decreases with age.
    B. Maximum heart rate increases with age.
    C. Pulse rate increases with age.
    D. The heart wall thickens with age.

15. Which of the following is TRUE?

    A. The proportion of immature sperm decreases with age.
    B. Sperm counts decline with age.
    C. Prostate size enlargement tends to occur after age 60.
    D. Relative frequency of sexual activity varies greatly with age.

16. Which of the following does NOT change differently between the sexes with age?

    A. Bone loss
    B. Hearing loss
    C. Heart wall thickening
    D. Oxygen capacity

17. Which of the following states provides the best chance of survival to age 100?

    A. Alaska
    B. Hawaii
    C. Louisiana
    D. Mississippi

18. Following a transient ischemic attack, paralysis of the face may occur, known as   18.____

    A. aphasia   B. diplopia
    C. paresis   D. quadriplegia

19. Kidney function affects drug   19.____

    A. absorption   B. activity
    C. distribution   D. metabolism

20. Reduction of lean body mass affects drug   20.____

    A. absorption   B. activity
    C. distribution   D. metabolism

21. Which types of exercise are sometimes not recommended for older individuals as they   21.____
    may stimulate the vasovagal response, increasing blood pressure?

    A. Aerobic   B. Anaerobic   C. Isometric   D. Kegel

22. Which exercise is sometimes prescribed for urinary incontinence?   22.____

    A. Aerobic   B. Anaerobic   C. Isometric   D. Kegel

23. Which of the following are recognized problems with the current structure of long-term   23.____
    care?
    I. Fragmented resources
    II. Gaps in services
    III Multiple funding sources
    The CORRECT answer is:

    A. I, II   B. I, III   C. II, III   D. I, II, III

24. In _____, a person or institution is designated to take over and protect the interests of a   24.____
    person judged to be incompetent.

    A. conservatorship   B. intervivos trust
    C. joint tenancy   D. power of attorney

25. Which of the following are the most significant factors regarding one's propensity to be a   25.____
    victim of crime?
    I. Age
    II. Income level
    III. Location
    The CORRECT answer is:

    A. I, II   B. I, III   C. II, III   D. I, II, III

KEY (CORRECT ANSWERS)

1.	B	11.	B
2.	C	12.	A
3.	D	13.	A
4.	D	14.	D
5.	C	15.	C
6.	D	16.	D
7.	A	17.	B
8.	C	18.	C
9.	A	19.	D
10.	A	20.	C

21. C
22. D
23. D
24. A
25. C

EXAMINATION SECTION
TEST 1

DIRECTIONS: Each question or incomplete statement is followed by several suggested answers or completions. Select the one that BEST answers the question or completes the statement. *PRINT THE LETTER OF THE CORRECT ANSWER IN THE SPACE AT THE RIGHT.*

1. Senior centers that serve older persons should meet the important needs of these individuals.
   Of the following, it would be LEAST appropriate for such centers to meet the need for

   A. full-time employment by acting as a placement bureau for center members
   B. modified physical activity to help keep older people active and prevent physical deterioration
   C. social activity to help aging people make friends and avoid isolation
   D. program activities in which older people may do volunteer service in hospitals or in the community

   1._____

2. Social group work is BEST defined as a method of social work which

   A. assigns people to groups for intensive psychotherapy as a means of crisis intervention
   B. helps people improve their social functioning and ability to cope with inter-personal problems
   C. utilizes unskilled community people to take over many social work organizations
   D. relies on the leader's ability to mobilize people into effective instruments for community reform

   2._____

3. Some recreation departments operate multi-service senior centers which provide social services related to nutrition, health needs, legal, or housing assistance, as well as recreation.
   This type of program is regarded by leading authorities in the field of recreation as

   A. usually *not* the function of a recreation department since it has proved to be a hindrance to customary social and recreational programs
   B. clearly *not* the function of a recreation department and should be discontinued
   C. an *appropriate* function of a recreation department and is justified by federal funding guidelines in this field
   D. an *appropriate* function of a recreation department only when the program is receiving a grant from the state department of aging

   3._____

4. The three MAJOR areas of social work training and practice are:

   A. Group work, psychiatric case work, and neighborhood management
   B. Community analysis, case work, and agency supervision
   C. Group rehabilitation, psychiatric community development, and case work
   D. Case work, group work, and community organization

   4._____

5. Geriatrics is becoming an increasingly important branch of medicine.
   Of the following, this is CHIEFLY due to

   A. greater specialization within the medical profession
   B. the discovery of penicillin and aureomycin

   5._____

C. advances in medical education
D. the increase in the span of life

6. The BASIC principle underlying a social security program is that the government should provide

    A. aid to families that is not dependent on state or local participation
    B. assistance to any worthy family unable to maintain itself independently
    C. protection to individuals against some of the social risks that are inherent in an industrialized society
    D. safeguards against those factors leading to economic depression

7. Of the following statements, the one which BEST describes the federal government's position, as stated in the Social Security Act, with regard to tests of character or fitness to be administered by local or state welfare departments to prospective clients is that

    A. no tests of character are required, but they are not specifically prohibited
    B. if tests of character are used, they must be uniform throughout the state
    C. tests of character are contrary to the philosophy of the federal government and are to be considered illegal
    D. no tests of character are required, and assistance to those states that use them will be withheld

8. One of the criticisms levelled against the program of medical assistance for the aged is that it

    A. receives more federal and state reimbursement than the Old Age Assistance program
    B. does not include persons who formerly received hospital care at total city expense
    C. is unnecessarily restrictive and requires a full welfare scrutiny of the resources of the applicant and his relatives
    D. requires careful documentation that a costly medical condition exists

9. Statistics of Old Age Assistance as administered by the Department of Social Service indicate that

    A. both the number of people needing assistance and the amount of money needed is *decreasing*
    B. both the number of people needing assistance and the amount of money needed is *increasing*
    C. the number of people needing assistance is *decreasing* and the amount of money they need is *increasing*
    D. the number of people needing assistance is *increasing* and the amount of money they need is *decreasing*

10. The one of the following factors which is MOST important in *preventing* persons 65 years of age and older from getting employment is the

    A. high premium rates which must be paid by employers to private retirement systems for employees in this age group
    B. lack of skill in modern industrial techniques of persons in this age group
    C. social security laws restricting employment of persons in this age group
    D. unwillingness of persons in this age group to continue supporting themselves

11. A social investigator becomes aware that a client receiving Old Age Assistance is spending some of the public assistance money received in a manner different from the way it was budgeted. She is regularly spending on entertainment about one-fourth of the money budgeted for food. This client is considered mentally and physically competent to handle money. There is no reason to suspect that the client has any unrevealed source of income.
   In such a case, the social investigator should USUALLY

   A. call upon the services of a homemaker to assist the client in spending the money as it was budgeted
   B. explain the budget to the client and explain that the case must be closed unless the budget is adhered to
   C. educate the client in the meaning and purpose of the budget but take no further action at this time
   D. reduce the allowance by an amount equal to that not used for budgeted needs

11.____

12. In administering the Social Security Act, it has been a tenet of the Social Security Administration that public assistance to needy people is a

   A. charitable gift
   B. gift insofar as the recipient is concerned but in the public interest because of its stimulus to business
   C. grant to which the people are entitled as a matter of right
   D. privilege to be accorded to worthy citizens

12.____

13. A recipient of Old Age Assistance notifies his social investigator that he expects to leave town for a two-months' visit with his daughter in Vermont.
    For the social investigator to tell the client that he will lose assistance during the period would be

    A. *correct;* recipients of public assistance must be discouraged from taking costly trips except in cases of visits to extremely ill, very close relatives
    B. *correct;* the recipient may lose all rights to receive assistance if he leaves the state for a period exceeding one month
    C. *incorrect;* the recipient may continue to receive assistance if temporarily absent from his legal residence (for a period up to six months) if he cannot meet his needs and is otherwise eligible
    D. *incorrect;* the recipient will receive assistance from the state of Vermont during that period under a mutual assistance law between the two states

13.____

14. With the establishment of insurance and assistance programs under the Social Security Act, many institutional programs for the aged have tended to the GREATEST extent toward an *increased* emphasis on providing, of the following types of assistance,

    A. care for the aged by denominational groups
    B. care for children requiring institutional treatment
    C. recreational facilities for the able-bodied aged
    D. care for the chronically ill and infirm aged

14.____

15. According to studies made by HEW, the benefits received by beneficiaries of the old age and survivors insurance program during past years

    A. were too small to be basically helpful
    B. represented about a third of the resources of most beneficiaries
    C. were an unimportant factor in income maintenance
    D. constituted the major portion of the family's income

16. Congress has adopted an amendment to the Social Security Act in regard to old age and survivors insurance benefits that affected the administration of public assistance, but deleted from the bill prior to enactment a section designed to

    A. extend the option of state governments to enter into agreements with the federal government to cover certain members of state retirement systems if two-thirds of the members elected to be covered
    B. increase the benefits of old-age insurance beneficiaries now on the rolls by $5 or 12 1/2%, whichever is larger, according to a conversion table based on total earnings after 1936
    C. increase benefits of persons who will retire in the future by raising the percentage in the formula applicable to the first $100 of the average monthly wage
    D. increase proportionately the benefits for wives, widows, children, and other categories of beneficiaries, subject to a limitation on benefits payable to a single family

17. Of the following terms, the one which BEST describes the Social Security Act is

    A. enabling legislation   B. regulatory statute
    C. appropriations act   D. act of mandamus

18. An old-age recipient who is partially incapacitated informs a worker on your staff that, while he is living in his son's home, the children in the family upset him and he has decided that he must have more peaceful living arrangements. He would like to live in a small boarding home which will offer simple physical conveniences and service such as he needs. A neighbor has a home in which he could live in a boarding arrangement, but up to this time, boarders have never been taken in there. He asks whether such an arrangement could be made and assistance continued.
    In such a situation, it would be PROPER to advise the old-age recipient that

    A. the home will have to be inspected by the department of housing and buildings and a permit issued
    B. the boarding home will have to be inspected and licensed by the department of health
    C. the department of social service will arrange for the home to be visited and evaluated as to housing standards
    D. he can make his own arrangements to live where he wants since he receives an unrestricted grant

19. An aged person who is unable to produce immediate proof of age has made an application for old-age assistance. He states that it will take about a week to obtain the necessary proof and that he does not have enough money to provide meals for himself until then.
    If it appears that he is in immediate need, he SHOULD be told that

    A. the law requires proof of age before any assistance can be granted

B. temporary assistance will be provided pending the completion of the investigation
C. a personal loan will be made to him from a revolving fund
D. he should arrange for a small loan from private sources

20. One of the following disclosures is made regarding an applicant for old age assistance, and he is accordingly disqualified to receive the grant requested.
In the recommendation submitted by the social services worker, the applicant would be found *ineligible* because he

    A. is not a citizen
    B. has $100 in a bank account which he is saving for burial purposes
    C. has three married children and could probably live with one of them
    D. refuses to give information concerning a bank account of $5000 which had been in his name until four months prior to his application

21. Geriatrics is the study of the problems of the

    A. aged
    B. institutionalized insane
    C. inmates of prison
    D. behavior of infants

22. Which one of the following provisions of the Social Security Act is administered by the federal government EXCLUSIVELY?

    A. Old-age assistance
    B. Old-age and survivors insurance
    C. Unemployment compensation
    D. Assistance for dependent children

23. The index number of consumer prices computed by the Bureau of Labor Statistics

    A. is frequently criticized because so few prices are taken into consideration
    B. avoids the use of a base year
    C. is a weighted index number
    D. is the average of the prices of many commodities

24. One approach to counseling of the aged has been labeled *non-directive*.
The word *non-directive* derives from the fact that, in this approach to counseling, the counselor

    A. does not tell the client what he should do
    B. makes the client responsible for the direction of the course of the interviews
    C. does not make judgments about the behavior of the client
    D. avoids possible areas of threat to the client

25. Of the following, the unique kind of assistance which group counseling provides for socially maladjusted senior citizens is

    A. the opportunity for the senior citizen to identify with a stable adult citizen
    B. the special type of social environment which the counseling group affords the senior citizen
    C. the senior citizen's growing conviction that he has been *chosen* for the group
    D. a lightened work load to compensate for the time and energy used in the group

KEY (CORRECT ANSWERS)

1. A
2. B
3. C
4. D
5. D

6. C
7. A
8. C
9. B
10. A

11. C
12. C
13. C
14. D
15. D

16. A
17. A
18. D
19. B
20. D

21. A
22. B
23. C
24. B
25. B

EXAMINATION SECTION
TEST 1

DIRECTIONS: Each question or incomplete statement is followed by several suggested answers or completions. Select the one that BEST answers the question or completes the statement. *PRINT THE LETTER OF THE CORRECT ANSWER IN THE SPACE AT THE RIGHT.*

1. Of the following groups of people, the one that might have the GREATEST difficulty in eating a diet with an adequate intake of protein is

    A. lacto-ovo-vegetarians
    B. strict vegetarians
    C. fruitarians (allow only fruits, seeds, nuts)
    D. lacto-vegetarians

    1.____

2. Of the following diet prescriptions ordered by a physician for patients, the one that should alert the dietitian to the need for a conference with the physician to discuss the feasibility of the prescription is

    A. 60 grams protein, 2 grams sodium, 2 grams potassium
    B. 1200 calories, fat controlled, Diabetic
    C. 125 grams protein, 500 milligrams sodium
    D. 1500 calories, 1 gram sodium, Liquid

    2.____

3. A hospitalized patient should be encouraged to participate in his own nutritional care. Of the following, the MOST effective tool the dietitian can use to initiate patient involvement is the

    A. selective menu
    B. diet history
    C. home diet instruction
    D. printed diet information sheet

    3.____

4. The one of the following which would be *inadvisable* for a dietitian to choose when requisitioning supplementary beverages for a patient on a potassium-restricted diet is

    A. orange juice   B. tomato juice
    C. apricot juice   D. apple juice

    4.____

5. Of the dietary recommendations issued by the American Diabetes Association, the MOST important objective in planning the diabetic diet is

    A. restriction of cholesterol and saturated fat
    B. de-emphasis of the traditional carbohydrate restriction
    C. control of caloric intake to achieve ideal body weight
    D. spacing of meals to minimize hyperglycemia

    5.____

6. Providing an optimum caloric intake for the patient on a protein-restricted diet presents a major problem to the dietitian when planning a home diet for the patient.
   Of the following suggestions, the one that should BEST help solve this problem is to *increase* the patient's intake of

    A. bread and cereals   B. sugar and fat
    C. vegetables and fruits   D. meat and poultry

    6.____

7. The Recommended Dietary Allowance of the National Research Council is a valuable tool for the dietitian which lists quantities of nutrients which

   A. cover therapeutic nutritional needs of individuals
   B. are normally required by adult males and females, but not by children
   C. are adequate to meet the known nutritional needs of most healthy persons
   D. are revised approximately every 10 years

8. Recent surveys of the nutritional status of hospitalized patients have shown that many patients can be classified as malnourished.
   Of the following activities, the one which is of MOST value to the dietitian in determining whether a patient is malnourished is

   A. recording the patient's height and weight
   B. questioning the patient about past food habits
   C. recording the patient's food consumption in the hospital
   D. assessing the results of routine laboratory examinations

9. Of the following items of information obtained from the patient during the diet interview, the one which would be of LEAST importance to the dietitian when planning a diet program with the patient is the

   A. amount of food consumed
   B. method of food preparation
   C. frequency of meals
   D. age of the patient

10. Of the following, the MOST critical factor involved in planning a diet program with a patient is

    A. accuracy of calculations of amounts of foods allowed
    B. obtaining acceptance of the diet program by the patient
    C. meeting the patient's budgetary allowances
    D. construction of a well-balanced diet

11. Assume that you have been counseling a young diabetic outpatient with a history of frequent hospital admissions for diabetic acidosis. In an attempt to evaluate your success, you reveiw her medical record for the past few months.
    Which of the following items indicates a successful teaching-learning process? The

    A. patient has not lost any weight
    B. patient's personal food records show a well-balanced, adequate intake
    C. patient has not been admitted to the hospital for three months
    D. results of the patient's current laboratory studies fall within normal limits

12. One of the dietitian's concerns is to bring about changes in patients' food habits, where necessary.
    The one of the following techniques which is MOST effective in bringing about such changes is

A. using audio-visual aids to illustrate good nutrition
B. giving individual instruction in principles of nutrition
C. lecturing on good nutrition to groups of patients
D. discussing patients' nutrition problems on an individual basis

13. The hospital dietitian is responsible for recording information relating to the patient's health care on the patient's medical chart.
Of the following, the item that is NOT considered appropriate for recording is the

    A. estimation of daily food intake
    B. comment on dietary restrictions which are unacceptable to the patient
    C. criticism of patient care by other disciplines
    D. request for patient referral to a community agency for diet follow-up at home

14. Suppose that you are preparing a written memo in order to inform your subordinates of a partial change in a work procedure.
Of the following, the clearest way to convey this information is to put in the memo

    A. only the part of the procedure that is changed
    B. the complete old and new procedures
    C. the complete new procedure, incorporating the change
    D. the complete old procedure, and the part that is changed

15. If you are writing a report on the feasibility of changing a dietary procedure which will be read by an administrator, the one of the following which would be BEST for you to do is to make the report

    A. very detailed, including all the minute facts available, thus enabling him to come to his own conclusions
    B. concise, giving him the main facts and your basic conclusions
    C. detailed, giving him all the available information and every possible conclusion
    D. concise, giving him the bare facts, thus enabling him to come to his own conclusions

---

KEY (CORRECT ANSWERS)

1. C	6. B	11. C
2. C	7. C	12. D
3. A	8. B	13. C
4. B	9. D	14. C
5. C	10. B	15. B

EXAMINATION SECTION
TEST 1

DIRECTIONS: Each question or incomplete statement is followed by several suggested answers or completions. Select the one that BEST answers the question or completes the statement. *PRINT THE LETTER OF THE CORRECT ANSWER IN THE SPACE AT THE RIGHT.*

1. Nonroutine, nonpredictable occurrences which cause difficulties in assessing staff requirements do NOT include

    A. unexpected physician's visits and orders
    B. patients going *sour*
    C. observation of previously unidentified patient needs
    D. none of the above

2. In the manpower planning process, one should NOT

    A. analyze the present supply situation by making an inventory of the work force
    B. analyze the short-term demand situation only
    C. evaluate and update the manpower forecast
    D. reevaluate and update the manpower forecast periodically

3. Techniques for measuring a nurse's activities do NOT include a(n)

    A. time study and task frequency study
    B. work sampling of nurse activity
    C. continuous observation of nurses performing activities
    D. estimate based on other nurse's activities

4. The objectives of scheduling and allocation procedures are to assign working days and days off to individual members of the nursing staff so that

    A. adequate patient care is ensured while overstaffing is avoided
    B. a desirable distribution of days off is achieved
    C. individual members of the nursing staff are treated fairly
    D. all of the above

5. All of the following are factors that should play a part in scheduling decisions EXCEPT

    A. the different levels of nursing staff
    B. nursing coverage should be provided for at least five working days
    C. weekend days off are highly prized by nursing staff
    D. despite a salary differential, evening and night shifts are more difficult to staff

6. A scheduling system can be assessed by observing how well it functions in terms of all of the following EXCEPT

    A. coverage   B. quality   C. quantity   D. stability

7. The ability of a scheduling system to handle changes is its

    A. coverage   B. flexibility
    C. quality   D. cost

8. The measure of a schedule's desirability as judged by the nurse who will have to work it is called its

   A. quality B. coverage C. quantity D. flexibility

9. The number of nurses assigned to be on duty is in relation to the minimum number of nurses required.
   This is called

   A. coverage B. flexibility C. fairness D. stability

10. The guidelines for good scheduling do NOT include that

    A. the schedule should represent a balance between the needs of the employee and the employer
    B. the schedule should distribute only *bad* days off among all employees
    C. all employees should adhere to the established rotation
    D. advance posting of time schedules allows employees to plan their personal lives

11. All of the following are constraints that cause difficulties in making schedules EXCEPT

    A. the number of weekends off - 1 in four, 1 in three, or every other weekend
    B. no maximum length of consecutive days worked
    C. whether days off should be together or split
    D. payroll and overtime considerations

12. All of the following are true about scheduling EXCEPT

    A. there is no one schedule that will work for all hospitals and all departments
    B. select several different schedules that complement each other and develop the best cyclical schedule for your department
    C. do not experiment with a combination of different schedules
    D. giving more or less of one variable affects the ability to give more or less of the others

13. The line functions for which the nurses in management positions should be responsible do NOT include

    A. establishing and controlling the personnel budget
    B. developing procedures for adjustment of staff on a daily basis
    C. primary care responsibility for a patient
    D. hiring, promoting, disciplining, and discharging employees

14. The staff functions for which the central scheduling office is responsible do NOT include

    A. gathering facts and preparing reports for line personnel to facilitate budgeting
    B. hiring and discharging staff
    C. implementing procedures for position control
    D. maintaining records needed by line managers for evaluation

15. One of the drawbacks of decentralized scheduling is that

    A. nurses have more input into staffing patterns
    B. the responsibility for staffing is entrusted to the unit supervisor
    C. the unit supervisor is not an expert in staffing methods
    D. the unit supervisor is aware of the clinical needs and personal needs of staff nurses

16. To implement a self-scheduling system, the head nurse sets up a series of meetings to   16.____

    A. identify problems with the existing scheduling system
    B. present self-scheduling as an alternative system
    C. establish a few practice sessions with self-scheduling
    D. all of the above

17. The following are true regarding employees working under a total flextime arrangement   17.____
    EXCEPT

    A. they may come and go as they please
    B. their work should be dependent on the work of others
    C. they need only to put in whatever total hours required of them for the work week
    D. they are required to accomplish the work expected of them

18. A flextime arrangement that allows workers the option of establishing their own starting   18.____
    and quitting times is called

    A. total flextime   B. team flextime
    C. limited flextime   D. job sharing

19. Two or more people working part-time and mutually arranging their schedules so as to fill   19.____
    one single position is called

    A. mutual flextime   B. total flextime
    C. job sharing   D. team flextime

20. One MAJOR advantage of the traditional approach to scheduling is   20.____

    A. stability   B. flexibility   C. coverage   D. quality

Questions 21-25.

DIRECTIONS: In Questions 21 through 25, match the nursing management positions in Column I with their respective job description.

                    COLUMN I
                A. Nursing service director
                B. Assistant nursing service director
                C. Supervisor nurse
                D. Head nurse
                E. Clinical nurse specialist

21. Direct and supervise nursing staff in provision of nursing care and ensure the availability   21.____
    of support services which facilitate this care.

22. Assist in organizing and administering the department of nursing.   22.____

23. Supervise and coordinate activities of nursing personnel engaged in specific nursing services.   23.____

24. Organize and administer the department of nursing.   24.____

25. Does not have authority over the other personnel, often responsible to nursing service   25.____
    director.

KEY (CORRECT ANSWERS)

1. D
2. B
3. D
4. D
5. B

6. C
7. B
8. A
9. A
10. B

11. B
12. C
13. C
14. B
15. C

16. D
17. B
18. C
19. C
20. B

21. D
22. B
23. C
24. A
25. E

TEST 2

DIRECTIONS: Each question or incomplete statement is followed by several suggested answers or completions. Select the one that BEST answers the question or completes the statement. *PRINT THE LETTER OF THE CORRECT ANSWER IN TEE SPACE AT THE RIGHT.*

1. The advantages of computer-aided traditional scheduling include

    A. the flexibility of the traditional approach
    B. reducing operating costs considerably
    C. producing high-quality schedules consistently
    D. all of the above

1.____

2. Cyclical scheduling, once established, has all of the following advantages EXCEPT

    A. it meets everyday staffing requirements
    B. the amount of highly skilled professional time spent on scheduling functions is reduced
    C. the *good* and *bad* days off are spread equitably among all employees
    D. schedules are known in advance by each employee

2.____

3. Disadvantages of the traditional approach to scheduling do NOT include

    A. rigidity   B. uneven coverage
    C. poor quality   D. instability

3.____

4. Disadvantages of a cyclical approach to scheduling include

    A. low quality   B. uneven coverage
    C. inflexibility   D. instability

4.____

5. The MAJOR disadvantage of a cyclical approach to scheduling is

    A. high cost   B. rigidity
    C. uneven coverage   D. time consumption

5.____

6. Which of the following is an ADVANTAGE of an 8-hour shift schedule?

    A. It does not allow staff to have every other weekend off.
    B. It does not permit the employee to have several consecutive days off.
    C. The body does not have to adjust to an extended work day.
    D. It results in unsafe traveling times

6.____

7. Advantages of a 10-hour shift schedule do NOT include that

    A. it allows for several consecutive days off
    B. it requires more employees than 8-hour and 12-hour shift schedules
    C. employees can have more weekends off
    D. individuals on different shifts have an opportunity to work together

7.____

8. The principal benefits of the seven on - seven off shift include

   A. increased utilization of space and equipment
   B. improved service to patients
   C. greatly reduced absenteeism
   D. all of the above

9. To overcome understaffing, nursing departments should establish *sister* units - cross-training groups that are comparable and related.
   Examples of cross-training groups include

   A. labor, delivery, and postpartum care nurses, newborn nursery, pediatrics
   B. neonatal I.C.U. and pediatric I.C.U.
   C. intensive care unit, coronary care unit, and emergency care unit
   D. all of the above

10. Advantages of part-time work may include all of the following EXCEPT

    A. broadening an individual's horizons beyond home or school
    B. an increase in income
    C. a decrease in continuity of patient care
    D. ego satisfaction

11. Per diem nurses are hired by the hospital to work as needed.
    Advantages of per diem nursing include

    A. scheduling flexibility
    B. more money per hour than career or part-time nurses
    C. the opportunity to fill in when staff are needed to work
    D. all of the above

12. The first and most obvious advantage of using temporary help agencies is the

    A. quality of care
    B. cost
    C. stable supply
    D. reduced need for orientation

13. Basic areas that should be addressed while developing a staff reduction plan include

    A. indicators for decision regarding staff reduction
    B. options and alternative plans
    C. criteria for determining employees to be reduced
    D. all of the above

14. If time permits, staffing can be adjusted on a long-term basis through attrition.
    Such action can be difficult if

    A. the rate of attrition, department wide, is low
    B. the rate of attrition in a given unit is low
    C. the time to achieve reduction is short
    D. all of the above

15. The LAST step in downsizing the staff should be 15.____

    A. temporary early retirement
    B. elimination of management positions
    C. terminations
    D. attrition

16. If time allows, the FIRST step in downsizing staff should be 16.____

    A. termination
    B. attrition
    C. conversion of a number of full-time to part-time positions
    D. temporary early retirement

17. All of the following are true about the laying off of people as a measure of downsizing the staff EXCEPT 17.____

    A. it should be the last resort after all other attempts have been made
    B. employees should not be given a thorough explanation of the circumstances
    C. employees should be advised that as circumstances change, they will again be considered for employment
    D. employees should be fully informed about their unemployment status

18. The MAJOR characteristics of an effective, high quality, cost effective nursing department include 18.____

    A. delivery related features
    B. evaluation related features
    C. policy related features
    D. all of the above

19. Evaluation related features of the cost and quality effective nursing department include all of the following EXCEPT 19.____

    A. a consumer feedback mechanism
    B. supervisor and peer evaluations
    C. a working relationship between nurses
    D. a nursing question and answer program

20. A patient with many medications, IV piggybacks, and who requires hourly vital sign monitoring and/or hourly output monitoring, according to the patient's needs classification system, is the one who requires _____ nursing care. 20.____

    A. maximum   B. above average
    C. average   D. minimal

Questions 21-25.

DIRECTIONS: In Questions 21 through 25, match the nursing positions in Column I with their respective job descriptions.

COLUMN I
A. Staff nurse
B. Patient care technician
C. Nursing aid
D. Licensed practical nurse
E. Nursing assistant

21. Performs various patient care activities and related nonprofessional services necessary in caring for the personal needs and comfort of patients. 21.____

22. Renders professional nursing care to patients on an assigned unit. 22.____

23. Performs a wide variety of patient care activities and accomodative services for assigned hospital patients as directed by head nurse. 23.____

24. Works under direct supervision of a registered nurse. 24.____

25. Performs same job duties as nursing aid. 25.____

KEY (CORRECT ANSWERS)

1.	D	11.	D
2.	A	12.	B
3.	A	13.	D
4.	C	14.	D
5.	B	15.	C
6.	C	16.	B
7.	B	17.	B
8.	D	18.	D
9.	D	19.	C
10.	C	20.	A

21. C
22. A
23. D
24. B
25. E

EXAMINATION SECTION
TEST 1

DIRECTIONS: Each question or incomplete statement is followed by several suggested answers or completions. Select the one that BEST answers the question or completes the statement. *PRINT THE LETTER OF THE CORRECT ANSWER IN THE SPACE AT THE RIGHT.*

1. Which of the following have traditionally been the most frequently reviewed drug class among hospitals?   1.____

    A. Antibiotics
    B. Nitroglycerides
    C. Anticoagulants
    D. Opiates

2. Before deciding to undertake an in-depth study of a function or department, hospital management should keep in mind that these studies are typically _____ times more expensive than overview studies.   2.____

    A. 2-3   B. 4-7   C. 8-10   D. 10-15

3. Which of the following is NOT a responsibility of a hospital's medical staff?   3.____

    A. Making the final decision in appointing candidates to the medical staff
    B. Disciplining individual physicians whose practice patterns deviate from the norm
    C. Granting specific practice privileges to individual members of the medical staff
    D. Assuring the ongoing process of continuing medical education for the hospital's physicians

4. A hospital has received financing by means of a 30-year tax-exempt bond. Generally, the no-call period attached to this bond would be _____ years.   4.____

    A. 5   B. 10   C. 15   D. 30

5. Which of the following types of job evaluation programs are commonly used in hospital human resources management?   5.____
    I. Ranking
    II. Point method
    III. Predetermined grading
    IV. Factor comparison
    The CORRECT answer is:

    A. I only   B. I, IV   C. III only   D. II, IV

6. As care models move from indemnity to precertification, mandatory second-opinion, and large-case management to closed-panel HMO, each of the following changes occurs EXCEPT   6.____

    A. more indirect interaction between plan and provider
    B. greater control of utilization
    C. overhead cost and complexity increases
    D. net reduction in rate of medical cost increases

7. An average admitting employee at a medical center should handle _____ appointments each day.

   A. 10-25   B. 20-35   C. 40-55   D. 50-70

8. In hospital management engineering, the primary objective of methods improvement is to

   A. reduce human motion
   B. improve the flow of information
   C. reduce total labor input
   D. increase interdepartmental collaboration

9. The economic order quantity, or EOQ, of hospital materials is calculated using each of the following factors EXCEPT

   A. depreciation   B. ordering cost
   C. holding cost   D. unit cost

10. Most studies of horizontally integrated health care systems have revealed that the one true advantage to this type of organization is

    A. improved access to management expertise
    B. an increase in labor productivity through more efficient use of personnel
    C. improvement in quality through increased service volume for specialized personnel
    D. increased political power to deal with planning, regulation, and reimbursement issues

11. A significant disadvantage to the design/build approach to hospital design and construction is that

    A. bid packages are not competitively bid or negotiated
    B. short-run capital costs are relatively high
    C. the scope of the project is often poorly defined
    D. the owner has limited control over cost-cutting measures or construction standards

12. The basic types of skills developed in the training of a health care administrator include the following EXCEPT

    A. medical   B. social
    C. technical   D. conceptual

13. Under Medicare regulations, the capital costs of unrelated suppliers are excluded from reimbursement eligibility if

    A. capital equipment is leased or rented by the provider
    B. the equipment is on the provider's premises
    C. it is lumped together with other indirect costs
    D. the charge for capital equipment is separately stated

14. In managing a hospital's inventory, which of the following steps is typically performed LAST?

    A. Calculating reorder points
    B. Conducting physical inventories of each storage location

C. Establishing target turnover rates for each item and location
D. Calculating turnover rates for each location

15. Multiprovider systems in the United States have tended to rely on three models of governance. Which of the following is the most popular of these? 15._____

    A. Corporate model
    B. Joint venture
    C. Parent holding company
    D. Modified parent holding company (advisory boards)

16. Actual productivity among hospital staff members is typically measured in terms of 16._____

    A. number of specified objectives met per person
    B. total expenditure per output
    C. person-hours per output
    D. total community health

17. In multihospital health care systems, the biggest impact on staffing costs is 17._____

    A. the size of the system
    B. the institutional composition
    C. profit or nonprofit status
    D. the type of integration

18. Which of the following duties is NOT typically performed by members of the admitting department? 18._____

    A. Patient placement
    B. Information management
    C. Patient transportation
    D. Intake interviewing

19. A hospital learns that its employees have initiated the unionization process. Under federal law, the hospital is permitted to 19._____

    A. hold employee meetings within 24 hours of the election
    B. question employees about union matters and meetings
    C. discuss the position of the hospital with employees individually at their work areas
    D. ask employees how they intend to vote

20. The primary contribution of a hospital's purchasing department is to 20._____

    A. lower the price of goods and services acquired by the hospital
    B. handle payments to vendors
    C. determine which goods and services should be acquired by the hospital
    D. determine who is authorized to make purchases for the hospital

21. The main obstacle to labor cost containment in hospitals is typically 21._____

    A. lack of interdepartmental coordination
    B. cost-based reimbursement systems
    C. collective bargaining
    D. poor scheduling

22. Central sterile reprocessing in a hospital is typically the responsibility of the _____ program.

    A. environmental services
    B. materials management
    C. nursing
    D. clinical laboratory

23. According to the Center for Medicare and Medicaid Services, what chronic condition affects the greatest population of Medicare beneficiaries?

    A. Arthritis
    B. Diabetes
    C. High cholesterol
    D. High blood pressure

24. In a typical hospital organization, outpatient clinics are units within the

    A. medical staff and departments
    B. support services
    C. ancillary services
    D. nursing department

25. Which of the following is/are disadvantages associated with the formation of a management services organization (MSO)?

    A. Tax considerations
    B. The inhibition of physician recruitment
    C. Uncertain operating costs
    D. Restricted access to managed care

KEY (CORRECT ANSWERS)

1. A		11. D	
2. D		12. A	
3. A		13. C	
4. B		14. A	
5. D		15. C	
6. A		16. C	
7. C		17. D	
8. A		18. B	
9. A		19. C	
10. B		20. A	

21. B
22. B
23. D
24. D
25. A

TEST 2

DIRECTIONS: Each question or incomplete statement is followed by several suggested answers or completions. Select the one that BEST answers the question or completes the statement. *PRINT THE LETTER OF THE CORRECT ANSWER IN THE SPACE AT THE RIGHT.*

1. The most common mistake administrators make in the strategic planning process is to   1._____

    A. fail to make the necessary changes because they do not agree with the strategy's initial conception
    B. fail to develop and propose radical strategies
    C. fail to test the new strategy before full implementation
    D. assume that there is only one correct strategy for each goal

2. The potential benefits which drive physicians and hospitals to form physician-hospital networks include each of the following opportunities EXCEPT   2._____

    A. establishing some measure of tax-exempt status for participating physicians
    B. improving the recruitment and retention of physicians
    C. offsetting increased administrative overhead
    D. enhancing contract negotiation leverage

3. Which of the following is a typical quality assurance oversight committee?   3._____

    A. Cancer care   B. Credentials
    C. Appeals   D. Infection control

4. In the planning of health care facilities, it is important to remember that ideally, the facility should have at LEAST _____ distinct entrances for the different types of individuals who use the facility.   4._____

    A. 3   B. 4   C. 6   D. 10

5. Which of the following procedures in the facilities planning process is typically performed LATEST in the process?   5._____

    A. Working drawings   B. Master site planning
    C. Schematic drawings   D. Bidding

6. Medicare's definition of the *facility services* component of ambulatory surgical centers (ASCs) does NOT include   6._____

    A. diagnostic procedures directly related to the provision of surgical procedures
    B. blood
    C. prosthetic devices
    D. administrative costs

7. Quality-of-service measurements used by hospitals in their quality control programs typically emphasize the measurement of   7._____

    A. standards   B. inputs
    C. processes   D. outputs

8. Bed utilization management in a hospital is typically the responsibility of the _____ department.

   A. admitting
   B. nursing
   C. finance
   D. accounting

9. The primary DISADVANTAGE of using equity financing for hospitals is

   A. additional bureaucracy
   B. decreased net worth
   C. dilution of ownership interest
   D. removal of some management incentives

10. Which of the following steps in a hospital's strategic planning process typically requires the largest amount of time?

    A. Assessing the mission statement
    B. Developing organizational goals
    C. Developing the action plan
    D. Assessing internal and external environments

11. Typically, the financing process at a large hospital takes about

    A. 15-30 days
    B. 2-3 months
    C. 4-6 months
    D. 7-9 months

12. The classical theorists in hospital organization agree that

    A. middle management should be the primary decision-making level
    B. decisions should always be made at the highest level
    C. staff and management should always arrive at decisions after consulting together
    D. decisions should be made at the lowest level possible, as long as they represent good management

13. The disability plans operated by most hospital human resources departments typically begin at around _____ weeks.

    A. 14
    B. 26
    C. 40
    D. 52

14. A hospital's assessment reveals a stakeholder who has both a high potential for threat to the hospital and a high potential for cooperation. In general, the hospital should attempt to

    A. monitor the stakeholder
    B. defend against the stakeholder
    C. collaborate with the stakeholder
    D. involve the stakeholder in as many internal decisions as possible

15. Which of the following statements about the quality assurance process is TRUE?

    A. It emphasizes processes over people.
    B. Its way of achieving accountability is to organize teams.
    C. It is externally driven.
    D. It accepts variation in methods.

16. Which of the following is NOT a category of laboratory test established by the federal government regarding the complexity of test methodology?

    A. Waived tests
    B. Tests of little complexity
    C. Tests of moderate complexity
    D. Tests of high complexity

17. In multihospital systems, approximately what percentage of staffing costs are spent at the corporate and regional level, as opposed to the local or institutional level?

    A. 10   B. 20   C. 40   D. 60

18. Which of the following is/are ways in which receiving departments can contribute to the bottom line at hospitals?
    I. Invoice matching
    II. Negotiating fixed contract prices for items or groups of items
    III. Monitoring and documenting vendor performance
    IV. Adjusting the timing of payments to vendors

    The CORRECT answer is:

    A. I, II
    B. I, IV
    C. II, III, IV
    D. III, IV

19. What type of reimbursement mechanism is commonly used by managed care organizations to control health-care costs?

    A. Capitation
    B. Fee-for-service
    C. Prospective payment
    D. Retrospective payment

20. As a means of distributing materials in hospitals, exchange carts involve the primary advantage of

    A. greater control over the productivity and performance quality of the employees who fill the carts
    B. decreased consumption, of space
    C. decreased travel time over point-of-use replenishment system
    D. low capital costs

21. The term for a liquidity facility of a variable rate demand bond (VRDB) is typically _____ year(s).

    A. 1   B. 2   C. 3-5   D. 5-10

22. Members of a hospital's provisional medical staff

    A. are doctors with areas of specialization who consult with other staff members, and who do not have the privileges of treating and admitting patients
    B. do not frequently admit patients and do not have the full obligations of active staff membership
    C. have been recently appointed and have fewer privileges and responsibilities than attending staff, such as the inability to vote
    D. are only given privileges for a designated period of time

23. In most point-of-service (POS) health care plans, the difference between in-network and out-of-network coverage for services is typically _____ %.

   A. 5-10   B. 10-15   C. 20-40   D. 30-50

24. Which of the following is generally considered to be the most important instrument in a hospital's wage and salary administration?

   A. Job analysis
   B. Performance evaluation
   C. Job description
   D. Screening process

25. The record retention schedule of a hospital's clinical information department should take into account each of the following EXCEPT

   A. legal, regulatory, and accrediting requirements
   B. patient flow
   C. educational programs
   D. research activities

KEY (CORRECT ANSWERS)

1. C		11. B	
2. A		12. D	
3. D		13. B	
4. C		14. C	
5. D		15. C	
6. C		16. B	
7. D		17. D	
8. A		18. B	
9. C		19. A	
10. D		20. A	

21. C
22. C
23. C
24. C
25. B

TEST 3

DIRECTIONS: Each question or incomplete statement is followed by several suggested answers or completions. Select the one that BEST answers the question or completes the statement. *PRINT THE LETTER OF THE CORRECT ANSWER IN THE SPACE AT THE RIGHT.*

1. In multiprovider systems, the capital allocation process should focus on

    A. internal rate of return
    B. net present value
    C. capital asset pricing
    D. discounted cash flow

    1.____

2. Which of the following would NOT generally be considered an *internal* stakeholder in a hospital?

    A. Support staff
    B. Paraprofessional staff
    C. Nonmanagement medical staff
    D. Nonclinical managers

    2.____

3. Which of the following is a CEO's role in the planning of a health care facility?

    A. Approving change orders relating to construction
    B. Overseeing the control of the capital program budget
    C. Making plans for physical facility implementation as they affect the hospital's operating mode
    D. Discharging or delegating the ability to sign contracts

    3.____

4. If a patient is transferred from a hospital participating in Medicare's PPS to another hospital that participates in PPS, the transferring hospital is reimbursed on a _____ basis.

    A. total charge
    B. pro-rated charge
    C. per diem rate
    D. per-discharge

    4.____

5. Which of the following is an outcome measure of quality for a hospital?

    A. Pain management
    B. Documentation of care
    C. Nursing services
    D. Compliance with discharge plan

    5.____

6. Which of the following food-service subsystems in a hospital typically requires the highest inventory of supplies?

    A. Production
    B. Procurement
    C. Distribution/service
    D. Maintenance

    6.____

7. Prospective management of utilization applies to

    A. capitation and fee-for-service reimbursement
    B. referral services and institutional services

    7.____

101

    C. case review and pattern analysis
    D. inpatient care and large-case management

8. In a hospital's cost finding process, which of the following would be counted as a direct cost?

    A. Administration
    B. Housekeeping
    C. Room and board
    D. Depreciation

9. In the current market, the joint venture between a hospital and other providers is least likely to be popular among

    A. ambulatory surgery centers
    B. general hospitals
    C. HMOs
    D. specialized hospitals

10. Under Medicare regulations, which of the following is defined as a capital cost?

    A. Insurance on depreciable assets
    B. Service agreements involving lease or rental arrangements
    C. Interest expense on working capital loans
    D. General liability insurance

11. Which of the following is LEAST likely to be an objective of a management services organization (MSO)?

    A. Competing in the managed care arena
    B. Ensuring the continued survival of the hospital
    C. Establishing a large multispecialty medical group
    D. Strengthening relationships with physicians

12. The primary difference between a Registered Record Administrator (RRA) and an Accredited Record Technician (ART) at a hospital is that

    A. an RRA must be a graduate of an accredited health information management program at the baccalaureate level
    B. an RRA must pass the national certification examination of the American Health Information Management Association
    C. most ART degree programs are at the master's level
    D. ART training devotes special emphasis to the use of computer technology in information management

13. With the increase in multiprovider systems, it has been suggested that these systems should be governed on two levels. What are these two levels?

    A. Administrative and departmental
    B. Inputs and outputs
    C. Strategic and operational
    D. Core and ancillary

14. Usually, the purchase of a major capital item by a hospital will require that vendors submit

A. written quotations that will be evaluated by the purchasing department
B. formal sealed bids that will be opened publicly
C. a telephone price quotation
D. fixed contract prices for groups of items

15. In forming a nonprofit foundation, which of the following is typically done LAST? 15._____

    A. Preparing a professional services agreement
    B. Applying for tax-exempt status
    C. Preparing articles and bylaws
    D. Applying for a Medicare provider number

16. Each of the following is an important element of the job evaluation process in hospitals EXCEPT to 16._____

    A. establish a wage scale that incorporates differentials
    B. discourage the union organization process through improved employee satisfaction
    C. determine the relative worth of various jobs in the hospital
    D. correct pay inequities

17. A hospital faced with fixed debt service requirements typically attempts to contain costs in each of the following ways EXCEPT by 17._____

    A. increasing patient throughput
    B. increasing labor productivity
    C. raising rates
    D. decreasing supply costs through more effective purchasing

18. Hospitals that are dissatisfied with an intermediary's decision regarding a DRG assignment must request a review within _____ days after the date a claim is paid. 18._____

    A. 30   B. 60   C. 90   D. 180

19. In most hospitals, the most significant fault in the scheduling of services is the 19._____

    A. repetition of tasks during an 8-hour shift
    B. 7-day operations
    C. flow of information
    D. *peak load* syndrome

20. Which of the following is NOT a way in which hospital leadership might help the human resources staff to maintain their expertise in specialized functions while assuming a more integrated role? 20._____

    A. Providing opportunities for external education and professional affiliation
    B. Keeping human resources staff together in one block of offices to encourage unity
    C. Exposing human resources staff to top management and board members whenever possible
    D. Creating interdisciplinary work teams

21. Under the provisions of the Federal Tax Reform Act of 1986, bonds issued after 1985 21._____

    A. must be fixed-rate if they are tax-exempt
    B. may be advance refunded only once

C. must have a maturity period of 30 years
D. have a maximum no-call period of 15 years

22. What type of medical record segregates entries by departments i.e., nursing, laboratory, radiology, social services, and physician services?

    A. Problem-oriented
    B. Quantitative
    C. Source-oriented
    D. Integrated

23. In the development of a new health care facility, or of an addition to an existing facility, nursing units should be constructed to serve a range of _____ beds each.

    A. 8-16   B. 12-24   C. 32-40   D. 45-60

24. Which of the following outpatient services is most likely to be eligible for full cost reimbursement under Medicare?

    A. Diagnostic services
    B. Laboratory services
    C. Surgery
    D. Radiology

25. During the 1990s, the primary purpose of diversification in multihospital systems became

    A. control over the demand for services
    B. the generation of revenue
    C. the divestiture of unwanted facilities
    D. offering services that reduce hospital costs

KEY (CORRECT ANSWERS)

1. C
2. C
3. C
4. C
5. D
6. A
7. B
8. C
9. B
10. A
11. C
12. A
13. C
14. B
15. D
16. B
17. C
18. B
19. D
20. B
21. B
22. C
23. C
24. A
25. D

NURSING HOMES

CONTENTS

PART ONE: ASSESSMENT OF NEED: IS NURSING HOME CARE THE BEST ALTERNATIVE?	1
What Are Some of the Alternatives?	1
Where To Begin	4
PART TWO: SOME QUESTIONS ABOUT NURSING HOMES	5
What Is A Nursing Home?	5
What Kinds of Nursing Homes Are There?	5
Why Do People Live in Nursing Homes?	6
How Does Medicare and Medicaid Pertain to Nursing Homes	6
How are Nursing Homes Owned and Managed?	8
How are Nursing Homes Regulated?	8
What Do Nursing Homes Do For Patients?	9
Who Provides Care?	13
What Rights Do Patients Have?	14
PART THREE: CHOOSING A NURSING HOME	17
Planning Ahead	17
Consulting Others	18
Finding Out What Kind of Home Is Needed	18
Deciding on the Location	19
Locating Nursing Homes	19
Narrowing the Field	20
Visiting Nursing Homes	21
Meeting with Key Personnel	21
Checking with State Nursing Home Ombudsman	23
Touring the Home	23
Making Follow-up Observations	26
Checking Costs and Other Arrangements	27
Making the Decision	29
Making the Selection	29
Following up	30
What To Do When You Have A Complaint	30
PART FOUR: CHECKLIST	31
General Physical Considerations	32
Safety	33
Medical, Dental, and other Services	34
Pharmaceutical Services	34
Nursing Services	35
Food Services	35
Rehabilitation Therapy	36
Social Services and Patient Activities	36
Patients' Rooms	37
Other Areas of the Nursing Home	37
Financial and Related Matters	38

NURSING HOMES

PART ONE

Assessment Of Need: Is Nursing Home Care The Best Alternative?

When a person can no longer live independently, a decision must be made about the best alternative arrangement for care. Such a decision often must be made during a time of crisis—frequently when the patient is ready to leave the hospital after a serious illness or operation.

Changed care needs may arise because of many reasons. A person has a stroke and can no longer remain at home alone. Frequent falls cause broken bones, and the individual needs a more protective setting. Increased forgetfulness or a heart condition poses a potentially serious threat to the well-being of the individual and necessitates increased health supervision.

When an individual needs 24-hour care and supervision, a nursing home is probably the best answer. However, when a less intensive and less restrictive form of care will suffice, a mix of services and/or programs popularly called "alternatives to institutional care" may be more appropriate.

The first step is to find out—with the help of various experts—what level of care is actually needed, and then to determine what combination of services is required to meet this need. This is done through an assessment of needs: by the doctor to determine the medical needs; by the nurse to determine health and nursing needs; by the social worker to determine social needs; and by other experts such as the therapists (speech, physical, occupational) to determine any special needs. On the basis of these findings, a care plan is developed. The next step is to match the recommendations for care with appropriate services and programs in the community.

WHAT ARE SOME OF THE ALTERNATIVES?

While communities throughout the nation have made much progress in developing many different kinds of alternatives, not all

NURSING HOMES

of these services and programs are available in each community. So it is important to find out about what resources are available in your own community.

Descriptions of some of the alternatives that you might consider are:

Home Health Care covers a broad range of services that are brought to a person in his or her own home. It includes such services as:

- part-time skilled nursing care
- part-time services of home health aide and homemakers (made necessary by a patient's poor health)
- occupational therapy
- physical therapy
- speech therapy
- nutrition counseling
- some medical supplies and equipment

Home Health Aide Services are provided under the supervision of a professional therapist (who also assesses the person's needs and plans for the service to be provided).

A homemaker-home health aide carries out such tasks as assistance with bathing and dressing, meal preparation, light cleaning and laundry.

Chore Services include yard maintenance, snow shoveling and heavy cleaning, either alone or in combination with homemaker-home health aide services.

Home-Delivered Meals provide nutritious meals delivered to a person in his or her own home, if for some reason the person is unable to prepare meals. One or two meals a day may be provided. Most programs provide five meals a week, a few also provide meals on weekends.

Congregate (Group) Dining is where a nutritious noon meal is served to older persons at such sites as senior centers or schools. Participation in these programs affords the opportunity for social interaction and for planned social activities which may be offered by some of these programs before or after the meal. Many programs provide transportation.

Adult Day Health Care means an organized day program of therapeutic, social and health activities. Services are provided to adults with functional impairments, either physical or mental, for

NURSING HOMES

the purpose of restoring or maintaining the greatest capacity for self-care. Provided on a short-term basis, adult day health care serves as a transition from a health facility or home health program to personal independence. Provided on a long-term basis, it serves as an alternative to institutionalization in a nursing home in two ways: 1) when 24-hour skilled nursing care is not medically necessary; or 2) when institutionalization is viewed as undesirable by the individual or by his or her family.

Some Adult Day Care programs are primarily social in nature. Many of these programs provide some health supervision, establish linkages with community health facilities, or provide transportation to needed health services.

Transportation and Escort Services are provided through volunteer driver programs or special mini-bus services for elderly or handicapped persons who do not have private transportation or who are unable to use public transportation. Physical assistance is also provided to persons needing help in shopping, going to medical appointments, or for other activities.

Telephone Reassurance programs provide a daily contact for persons who live alone and who are anxious about their safety or security or have chronic health problems. Usually, the client calls a central switchboard at an agreed-upon time during the day. If no one answers a call placed to the home, the neighbors or the police are alerted to check on the person.

Friendly Visiting insures friendly contact made to persons who are isolated or homebound and do not have regular contact with relatives or neighbors. These visits are usually provided on a regular basis by volunteers from church groups or social agencies.

Protective Services provide legal and financial services and/or conservatorship (a type of guardianship) to mentally confused persons, and to others who are unable to manage their own affairs or protect themselves from injury or exploitation.

Elderly Foster Care is where a family or individual(s) share their home with an older person who is unable to live alone, usually due to a medical problem. Some states have programs which pay the foster family for giving care to an older person.

Congregate Living represents a shared living arrangement for several persons who can not live totally independently, but are able to live in a group, relying on the strengths each person can contribute to such tasks as cleaning, cooking and shopping.

NURSING HOMES

Sometimes, through pooling of funds, the group can afford to purchase housekeeping and cooking services that they could not afford if living in separate quarters.

Special Housing Arrangements are available in many communities for older or handicapped people. Many of these programs are for low and moderate income persons; some programs offer a variety of social and health-supportive services to the residents.

Hospice is a service, usually by a facility or at home, that provides supportive care for terminally ill patients (usually cancer victims) and their families, using an individualized plan of care approved by the family physician, especially to control and relieve pain. As needed, other kinds of home care are integrated into this service that is available on a 7 day a week, 24-hour basis.

Information and Referral services are designed to help the individual find where to obtain any of the needed services.

WHERE TO BEGIN

First, it is important to know about the facilities, programs, and services available in your community. You can be helped in this task by discussing the problem with the social services office of the community public welfare agency, the social worker in the hospital (if that is where the patient is at the time), or a social worker in any philanthropic or church-related social agency in your community. If there is a Information and Referral Service available in your community, this group can be of enormous help in providing guidance. The State Welfare Office (listed in the Appendix) can help you find your local welfare agency. Or you can contact your Area Agency on Aging for guidance. (The State Office on Aging, listed in the Appendix, can tell you where it is and give you the telephone number.)

Whenever possible, the assessment and planning process should involve all who are concerned—the individuals, the family, the physician, the social worker, and the clergyman.

As was mentioned earlier, many different types of care are now available to give you many more choices when long-term care problems arise. For some persons, however, nursing home care is the only answer to meet their needs. In those cases, the challenge is to find the most suitable nursing home for the individual and the family.

NURSING HOMES

PART TWO

Answers To Some Questions About Nursing Homes

WHAT IS A NURSING HOME?

In this guide, we use the term to mean a patient care facility that primarily provides nursing, medical, and rehabilitation care, but also furnishes residential and personal services as well.

Residential and personal services. These are the most basic services, ones that you would expect of most facilities for elderly people.

Residential care means providing a pleasant, healthful place to live—a comfortable room, nutritious meals, clean laundry, the services of a barber and beautician, and the companionship of others.

Personal care involves helping patients with such everyday tasks as dressing, bathing, toileting, eating and walking. It also includes certain kinds of supervision, such as helping patients to get to scheduled activities and therapy sessions, and helping them to follow prescribed programs of special diets and exercises.

WHAT KINDS OF NURSING HOME ARE THERE?

All facilities that can properly be called "nursing homes" do not offer the same level of care. Some homes specialize in personal care, while others specialize in health or nursing care. Others take care of residents with all kinds of needs—from help with eating to posthospital medical care. This situation became more clearly defined with the passage of Medicare and Medicaid legislation in the 1960's. These government programs established two categories of nursing homes (or long-term care facilities) according to the services they give:

> A *skilled nursing facility* (SNF) is a nursing home that has been certified as meeting Federal standards within the meaning of the Social Security Act. It provides the level of

NURSING HOMES

care that comes closest to hospital care with 24-hour nursing services. Regular medical supervision and rehabilitation therapy are also provided. Generally, a skilled nursing facility cares for convalescent patients and those with long-term illnesses.

An *intermediate care facility* (ICF) is also certified and meets Federal standards and provides less extensive health related care and services. It has regular nursing service, but not around the clock. Most intermediate care facilities carry on rehabilitation programs, with an emphasis on personal care and social services. Mainly, these homes serve people who are not fully capable of living by themselves, yet are not necessarily ill enough to need 24-hour nursing care.

Many nursing homes are certified to participate in both the Federal Medicare and Medicaid programs, and qualify as both skilled nursing facilities and intermediate care facilities.

WHY DO PEOPLE LIVE IN NURSING HOMES?

Many patients in nursing homes are old. Some are feeble and unable to take care of themselves and live safely on their own. Other patients, regardless of age, suffer from chronic illnesses and need some medical attention, but do not require hospital care. Still other patients have been transferred to the nursing home from a hospital to convalesce after a serious illness, accident or operation.

In recent years, nursing homes have received an increasing number of patients under the age of 65. Some of them are mentally retarded or have other developmental disabilities. Many of these younger persons as well as others have come to nursing homes from State mental hospitals. There are also a large number who are disabled war veterans or have permanent disabilities as the result of auto accidents or other trauma.

Some nursing home residents have no families. In other cases, the families are not able to supply the kind of care the individual needs—there may be no one home during the day, or the care needed may be too specialized or too expensive to provide at home. In still other cases, families may decide that keeping the person at home would upset family life too much.

HOW DO MEDICARE AND MEDICAID PERTAIN TO NURSING HOMES?

Created in 1965, these government programs are designed to help meet the health care needs and to help pay the bills of peo-

NURSING HOMES

ple over age 65 and the poor. Both programs include coverage for nursing home care. (It should be noted, however, that Medicare does not pay for care in an intermediate care facility.)

Medicare is a Federal program of hospital and medical insurance that applies to people over the age of 65, and also covers persons of all ages who have been disabled for at least two years or who have certain chronic renal disorders. It pays some of the cost of care in a skilled nursing facility. It covers a "spell of illness" of up to 100 days of care, but only after a stay of at least three days in a hospital. If care is needed beyond 100 days, the cost of care may be paid by Medicaid if the patient is eligible for such coverage. It is important to know that Medicare will not pay for care in a skilled nursing home unless the patient needs skilled nursing care or skilled rehabilitation services on a daily basis. Medicare cannot pay for care in an intermediate care facility, or for care in a skilled nursing home if the care needed is mainly custodial.

Care is considered custodial when it is primarily for the purpose of meeting personal needs and could be provided by persons without professional skills or training: Helping with such everyday tasks as walking, getting in and out of bed, bathing, dressing, eating, and taking medicine are considered custodial care.

Medicaid helps provide medical services to people with little or no income. The program is operated by the individual States (except for Arizona), although the Federal government provides up to 75 percent of the funds. Medicaid pays for care in both skilled nursing facilities and intermediate care facilities in all States (except Arizona); care in ICFs for the mentally retarded, is provided in most States. Since January 1, 1973, people who are medically needy share the cost of service they receive under Medicaid by paying a nominal enrollment fee or premium, based on the amount of the individual's income.

Medicare provisions change often, and Medicaid programs vary from State to State. For up-to-date information in your State, contact the local Social Security Office (for Medicare) or your State of local welfare office (for Medicaid). (Note: The telephone number for your local Social Security Office can be found in your telephone directory under U.S. Government. Addresses of the State welfare offices are listed in the Appendix.)

NURSING HOMES

HOW ARE NURSING HOMES OWNED AND MANAGED?

Some nursing homes are nonprofit institutions. They are sponsored by religious, charitable, fraternal and other groups or run by government agencies at the Federal, State or local levels. But most homes are private businesses, operated for profit. They may be owned by individuals or corporations. Sometimes they are part of a chain of nursing homes.

Final responsibility for the operation of a nursing home lies with its *governing body*. The governing body may be called the "board of directors" or "trustees," or they may be the owners of a proprietary facility. However they are constituted, they are the legal entity responsible for the home. The governing body meets periodically to set policies and to adopt and enforce rules and regulations for the health care and safety of patients.

The person in charge of the day to day management of a nursing home is called the *administrator,* and is appointed by the governing body. State licensing of the nursing home administrator is required.

HOW ARE NURSING HOMES REGULATED?

Nursing homes are required to meet standards set by State or local laws and regulations, and have a State license or letter of approval for a licensing agency to operate. *Participation by the nursing home in the Medicare and/or Medicaid programs is strictly on a voluntary basis.* Some nursing homes may choose to participate in only one program, and so are certified for that kind of program (Medicare or Medicaid); other nursing homes are certified for both Medicare and Medicaid. Payment for care in a nursing home by Medicare and Medicaid programs can be made only for care provided in certified facilities.

Nursing homes that are certified to take part in Medicare and Medicaid are required to meet standards set by Federal regulations. These standards are developed by the Bureau of Health Standards and Quality of the Health Care Financing Administration (HCFA), U.S. Department of Health and Human Services (DHHS).

HCFA is the agency responsible for continuing the Department's initiatives started in 1974 to improve the quality of care in long-term care facilities. As a part of this goal, a guide to patient care management has been developed which uses an integrated approach to patient care, and includes formal assessment of each patient's needs, a plan of care to meet those needs, and periodic evaluation of the outcomes of care.

NURSING HOMES

State agency or public health department surveyors evaluate homes periodically to make sure they meet health, safety, staffing and environmental standards, and that they are providing care that is consistent with the patient care management requirements.

WHAT DO NURSING HOMES DO FOR RESIDENTS

There is nothing about a nursing home that is more important than resident care. A home may be clean and well-equipped, but this means very little unless it also has a well-rounded program of good quality services for residents.

The goal of resident care in a nursing home is to provide care and treatment designed to restore and/or maintain the resident's highest level of physical and mental health.

Often nursing homes make arrangements with outside people to furnish certain services, such as rehabilitation therapy and consultation for dietary, social, activities and pharmaceutical needs.

The following pages describe some important aspects of care. (Additional points are covered in the checklist in Part Four.) Some of these points reflect Federal regulations for facilities participating in the Medicare and Medicaid programs. Others are simply good nursing home practices.

Food services. Residents should have meals that are nourishing, well-balanced, and appetizing. These meals should meet the daily nutritional needs of individual patients and should be properly scheduled. Residents should be offered nutritious snacks between meals and at bedtime. Some residents requrie special diets prescribed by their physicians. The facility should be able to provide such prescribed diets. Most often, food preparation takes place in the nursing home; in some cases, however, the nursing home makes arrangements with an outside company to provide food services. When you visit a nursing home, you will probably have a chance to meet the *food service supervisor* who is the person in charge of menu planning and food preparation. The kitchen staff should be large enough to prepare meals promptly and efficiently and under safe sanitary conditions. Hot foods should be served hot and cold foods cold.

Nursing services. In many ways, nursing care is what nursing homes are all about. Nursing personnel keep residents clean and comfortable, administer drugs, apply dressings and take steps to prevent pressure sores. They provide treatment to patients suffering from such problems as strokes, heart disease, and orthopedic illnesses who have been transferred from hospitals.

NURSING HOMES

When you visit a nursing home, you will see several kinds of people on the nursing staff:

A *registered nurse* (RN) is a licensed nurse, usually having completed basic preparation in a diploma, associate degree, or baccalaureate degree program in an accredited school of nursing that requires two to four years of study. RNs supervise nursing services, carry out various administrative duties, and, as required to meet patient's needs, they are able to give highly skilled nursing care.

A *nurse practitioner* is an RN with additional knowledge and skill gained through an organized nurse practitioner program of study and supervised practitioner experience. It is significant that after successfully completing graduate programs of study, an increasing number of professional nurses are awarded masters and doctoral degrees, and are thus prepared to assume broad nurse leadership and nursing care responsibilities.

A *licensed practical nurse* (LPN) usually has had at least one year of specialized training. Generally, LPNs do the less complex nursing jobs, with emphasis on bedside care. In California and Texas, an LPN is called a *licensed vocational nurse* (LVN).

Nurses' aides and *orderlies* work under the supervision of RNs and LPNs. They help residents get out of bed and get dressed in the morning, bathe them, make their beds, clean their rooms, bring their meals and feed them, and carry out similar kinds of personal care and housekeeping duties. Training of aides and orderlies is usually given by the nursing home.

Federal Regulations have very specific requirements for the nursing staff in nursing homes. These are covered in the checklist (Part Four.)

Physician services. Every resident in a nursing home must be under the care of a physician. A key role is played by the attending physician. He or she is responsible for the medical care of the individual patient—making the examination and diagnosis and prescribing the needed treatment, diet, drugs, and rehabilitation program. For the most part, the attending physician is the resident's own personal physician. In some cases, however, attending physicians are provided by the nursing home.

Federal regulations require that a skilled nursing facility must have a physician on its staff at least part-time to serve as medical

NURSING HOMES

director. The major functions of the medical director are: 1) coordinate all medical care for residents, 2) keep the quality of care under constant close watch, and 3) check on the health of the home's employees.

Federal regulations also set guidelines for visits by physicians. A resident must be given a physical examination just before or at the time he or she is admitted to the nursing home. Periodic follow-up visits should be made by the attending physician for continuous health management. In addition, good nursing homes bring in specialists to make regular checkups of residents' teeth, eyes, and feet. This is particularly important in care of the elderly.

Pharmaceutical services. Pharmaceutical services must be under the general supervision of a qualified pharmacist. A pharmacist reviews each resident's drug regimen regularly, and works with the physician and other facility staff to assure that each resident receives the right drug at the right time in the prescribed manner. Drugs are given to residents by qualified personnel, e.g., registered nurses, licensed practical nurses, or trained medication aides (under the supervision of a nurse).

Rehabilitation therapy typifies modern thinking about nursing home care. The principal aim is to help residents regain capabilities they have lost, allowing them to get along on their own as much as possible. Experience has shown that even the very elderly are often capable of great improvements.

Under Federal regulations, a nursing home may accept residents who are in need of specialized rehabilitation services only if it can provide or arrange for these special services.

Most nursing homes offer three types of rehabilitation therapy: *physical therapy, occupational therapy* and *speech/language pathology therapy.*

Physical Therapy. As a result of illness or injury, some people need help to regain lost abilities in body functioning. Physical therapists and their aides—using exercises, massages, and special training equipment—help residents to improve their abilities to sit, turn, stand, and walk or to carry on such everyday activities as eating, dressing and bathing. They also teach residents to use wheelchairs, braces, and artificial limbs.

When you visit a nursing home, you will probably see a special physical therapy room equipped with exercise equipment, whirlpool baths, and the like.

NURSING HOMES

Occupational Therapy. Occupational therapists work to develop occupational and recreational skills by involving residents in a variety of craft activities. These activities stimulate their interest and provide patients with a sense of satisfaction by accomplishing projects and by giving them practice in making precise movements of the hands and arms.

In large nursing homes, occupational therapy is usually carried on in a special room supplied with craft materials and equipment. In smaller homes, the dining room may double as an occupational therapy room.

Speech/Language pathology therapy. A speech/language pathologist helps residents overcome speech and language difficulties such as those due to stroke, hearing loss, or neuromuscular disorders. Speech/language therapy may be carried on in residents' rooms or in other areas of the home.

Social Services. Residents in nursing homes may have emotional concerns or problems and social adjustment difficulties. Sometimes these stem from entering the home itself: residents are separated from familiar people and places, their customary living patterns are disrupted, they are fearful of change and they become depressed. Sometimes the difficulties are connected with growing old, and feeling unwanted.

In recent years, we have come to realize more and more that nursing homes must deal with the whole person—not just with medical and physical needs, but with emotional and social ones as well. Nursing homes may not be required to offer social services themselves, but they are required to determine the social and emotional needs of the resident. If they do not provide these services to meet these needs, they must be able to refer residents and their families to outside agencies for assistance. If a home does provide social services, the person in charge is called the *director of social services*.

A good social service director tries to prepare people before they enter the home and help them adjust once they arrive. He or she counsels residents and their families, referring them to outside agencies for financial or legal help when necessary. When the time comes for residents to leave the nursing home, the director helps them and their families plan for the transition.

Reality Orientation: "Reality orientation" is a program which helps patients stay in contact with the real world by keeping them aware of the day and time of year, weather, holidays, activities in the home, and major news events.

NURSING HOMES

Patient activities. A suitable program of recreational activities in a nursing home is an important part of total care. Interesting and varied activities, supervised by a qualified activities coordinator, can do much to relieve the monotony of life and keep residents mentally alert, actively involved, and socially in contact.

Activities programs vary widely from one nursing home to another. Some homes have very limited programs. Others, particularly those with many active patients, have large and elaborate programs.

A well-rounded program may include individual activities (such as arts and crafts, reading, and letter writing), group activities (care games, billiards, exercise classes, drama and choral groups), noisy activities (rhythm bands, sing-alongs), highly social activities (dances, parties, birthday and holiday celebrations), outdoor activities (gardening classes, nature walks), and opportunities to get away from the home for a time (such as trips to parks, theaters, concerts, and museums).

Some nursing homes have book and record collections, movies, and discussion groups. Sometimes people from the community, such as librarians and theatrical groups, bring their services to the home. Some homes have a Resident Council which helps plan and carry on the activities program. A rich activities program is one of the hallmarks of a good nursing home, and you should inquire about it in any home you visit.

Volunteer program. A well-organized volunteer program can be a tremendous asset to a nursing home. Working and visiting with residents, community volunteers can help stretch a limited staff, increase the number of activities, and provide much needed contact with the outside world.

Religious observances. Many older people like to attend religious services and talk with clergymen. Nursing homes should provide opportunities to do so, whether in the home or at a nearby place of worship. Some homes have a chaplain and provide a chapel that is open for private meditation.

WHO PROVIDES CARE?

In a nursing home, each member of the staff plays a vital role in assuring that the resident receives a certain quality of care and services. The staff consists of administrative, professional, and non-professional personnel. The administrative staff is responsible for assuring that the facility operates effectively. Qualified health professionals, such as nurses, physicians, and dietitians,

NURSING HOMES

are responsible for assessing the needs of each resident and providing the necessary care. Professional staff are available to meet the medical, social, and emotional needs of each resident. The nonprofessional staff includes the aides and orderlies. These employees deliver many of the daily services directly to the residents in nursing homes.

Physicians, nurses, and other health personnel need to be attracted to providing long-term care in nursing homes. Today, education programs for health professionals frequently include both theory and practice in geriatrics and/or gerontology. These individuals will enter practice as better prepared and interested personnel.

WHAT RIGHTS DO PATIENTS HAVE?

Under Federal regulations, nursing homes must have written policies covering the rights of residents. They are required to make these policies available to residents and to the public. A kind of "bill of rights," the policies ensure that each resident admitted to the facility:

1. is fully informed, as evidenced by the resident's written acknowledgment of these rights and of all rules and regulations governing the exercise of these rights;

2. is fully informed, of services available in the facility and of related charges including any charges for services not covered under Medicare or Medicaid, or not covered by the facility's basic daily rate;

3. is fully informed, of his medical condition unless the physician notes in the medical record that it is not in the patient's interest to be told, and is afforded the opportunity to participate in the planning of his medical treatment and to refuse to participate in experimental research;

4. it transferred or discharged only for medical reasons, or for his welfare or that of other residents, and is given reasonable advance notice to ensure orderly transfer or discharge;

5. is encouraged and assisted, throughout his period of stay, to exercise his rights as a resident and as a free citizen. To this end he may voice grievances and recommend changes in policies and services to facility staff and/or to outside representatives of his choice without fear of coercion, discrimination, or reprisal;

NURSING HOMES

6. may manage his personal financial affairs, or is given at least a quarterly accounting of financial transactions made on his behalf if the facility accepts the responsibility to safeguard his funds for him;

7. is free from mental and physical abuse, and free from chemical and physical restraints except as authorized in writing by a physician for a specified and limited period of time, or when necessary to protect the patient from injury to himself or to others;

8. is assured confidential treatment of his personal and medical records, and may approve or refuse their release to any individual outside the facility;

9. is treated with consideration, respect, and full recognition of his dignity and individuality, including privacy in treatment and in care for his personal needs;

10. is not required to perform services for the facility that are not included for therapeutic purposes in this plan of care;

11. may associate and communicate privately with persons of his choice, and send and receive his personal mail unopened;

12. may meet with, and participate in activities of social, religious, and community groups at his discretion;

13. may retain and use his personal clothing and possessions as space permits, unless to do so would infringe upon rights of other patients, or constitute a hazard to safety;

14. is assured privacy for visits by his/her spouse; if both are inpatients in the facility, they are permitted to share a room.

NURSING HOMES

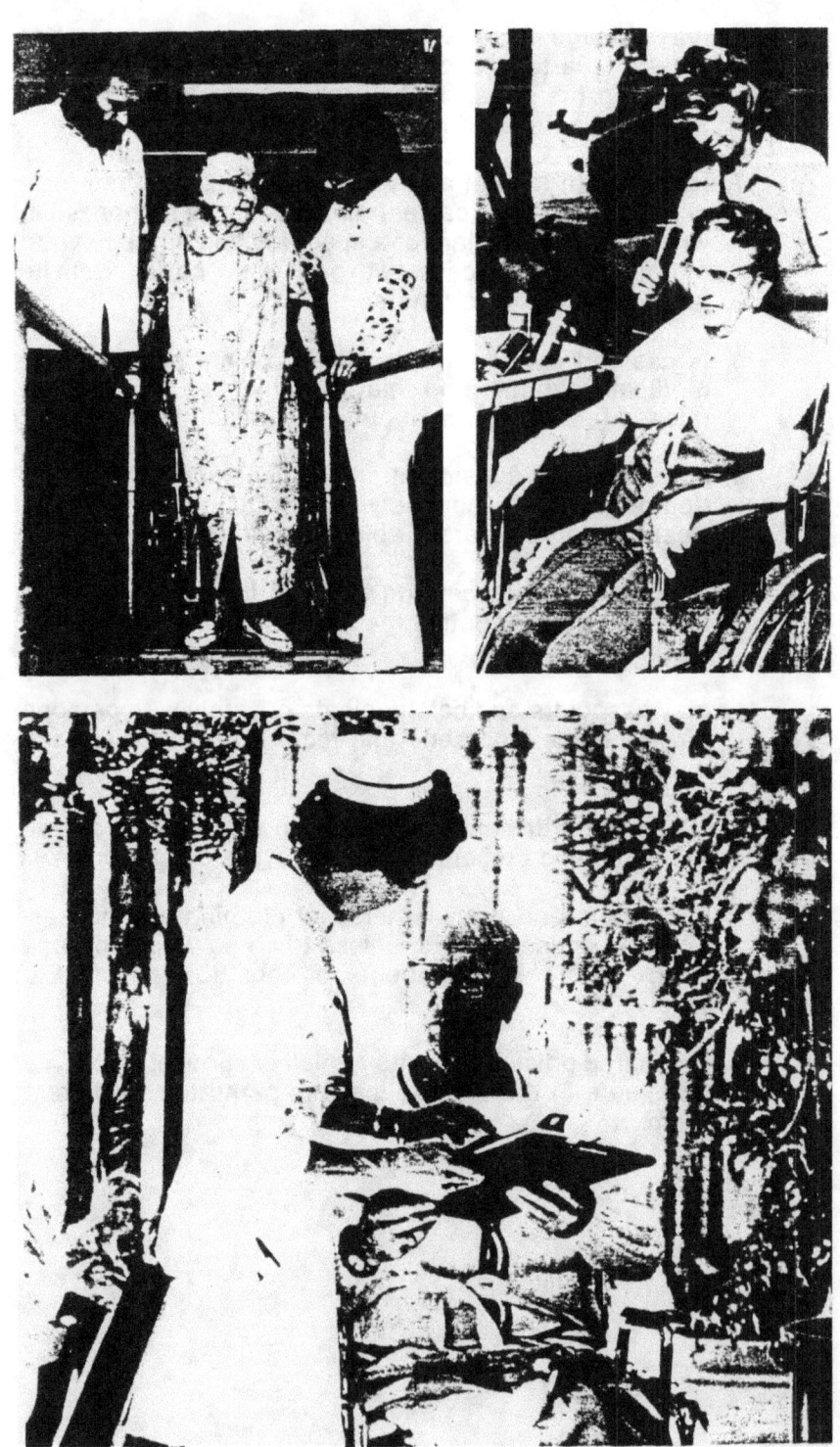

NURSING HOMES

PART THREE

Choosing A Nursing Home

PLANNING AHEAD. If you think you will need a nursing home at some time in the foreseeable future—for yourself or for an aging relative—it will pay to plan ahead. Many of the good nursing homes have long waiting lists, and chances of getting placement in the home of your choice may be greatly enhanced if placement is made on the waiting list prior to the actual time of need. Also this will give the prospective patient time to get mentally adjusted to the idea of the change.

Unfortunately, the choice of a nursing home is often made in a crisis atmosphere, when time is short and minds are troubled. But selecting a home is an important decision—one that deserves foresight and careful, clear-headed consideration.

Here are some things you can do in advance:

• Make a point of learning about nursing homes. In addition to reading this booklet, watch for articles in newspapers and magazines and for television programs that deal with nursing homes. Also, pick up brochures on the subject from social service agencies or your local health department.

• Find out what nursing homes are located in your community, and learn what you can about them. If you have friends or relatives who are familiar with the homes, ask for their opinions of them. If you know people who live in nursing homes, pay them a visit and gather some firsthand impressions.

NURSING HOMES

• Discuss the matter with the prospective patient, and find out his or her preferences.

• Think about ways of financing nursing home care. Find out whether the elderly person is likely to be eligible for Medicare or Medicaid or whether he or she has personal health insurance or a pension plan that covers nursing home costs. If not, begin planning other means of financing.

CONSULTING OTHERS. When the times comes to find a nursing home, other people can help. Consulting with the elderly person's physician is essential. Other physicians, social workers, clergymen, and friends or relatives who have placed someone in a nursing home can all offer valuable advice.

The person who will be entering the home should not be overlooked. If he or she is mentally alert, the person deserves to have his or her wishes considered and should be involved in the process of selecting the home every step of the way.

FINDING OUT WHAT KIND OF HOME IS NEEDED. The crucial question is: What kind of care does the elderly person need? Some may only require a safe and comfortable place to live, among pleasant companions. Some may want a home that places special emphasis on ethnic factors, such as special food or foreign languages; for some, there may be a preference for similarity in religious background. Others may need some help with grooming and occasional medical treatment. Still others may need constant medical attention, therapy, and other hospital-related care.

As discussed in the preceding section, different kinds of nursing homes provide different levels of care. The key is to match the home to the patient—to ensure the patient is in a home that provides the kind of care and services needed.

How can you find out what kind of care the person needs? The best source of guidance is his or her personal physician. When you talk to the physician, find out precisely whether an intermediate care facility or a skilled nursing facility can provide the level of care needed. Also ask about any special services or treatments that should be provided by the facility for the patient. (See p. 9).

NURSING HOMES

DECIDING ON THE LOCATION. In addition to finding out what *kind* of nursing home is needed, you should decide on a general location. In thinking about location, keep in mind that the most important goal is to provide the elderly person with the kind of care that is needed. Here are some points to consider:

• The location should be agreeable to the elderly person. For example, some people may prefer the restfulness of country surroundings, while others may prefer the stimulation of city life and being near community services such as those available from churches or community centers.

• The home should be convenient for the person's family and friends. Having to make a long trip may discourage people who would otherwise visit often.
• The home should be reasonably close to a hospital offering emergency service. In the event of an emergency, reaching a hospital quickly may be crucial.

• If the available homes in the local area cannot meet the patient's needs, you probably should go further away to get it.

LOCATING NURSING HOMES. The next step is to find out which nursing homes are available in the area you have in mind. Go over the list with your physician to ascertain which nursing homes he would recommend.

Some communities now have citizen groups which visit nursing homes, compile directories of homes, make digests of survey reports, and in general, try to protect the consumer's interests. If there is such a group near you, it should be consulted.

Many agencies and organizations keep lists of homes in order to make referrals to the public. (Usually, however, they do not make specific recommendations.) These are some places you might contact:

- Local or State health department
- Hospital, Social Services Department

NURSING HOMES

- Provider associations, i.e., State Health Care Nursing Home Associations, Association of Homes for Aging, etc.
- Local Office of the Social Security Administration
- Local Welfare Department
- Church groups
- Yellow pages of your telephone directory

In addition, you can often talk to individuals who are acquainted with the nursing homes in a given area—people like physicians, clergymen, relatives, and friends.

Make a list of the homes mentioned to you. Do not worry if the list is long; the more choices you have, the better your chances are of making a good selection.

NARROWING THE FIELD. You do not need to visit all the nursing homes on your list. Some can be eliminated simply by making telephone calls to the homes.

Here are some things to ask about:

Does the home provide the kind of care the elderly person needs? Is the home of the kind specified by the physician—a skilled nursing facility, intermediate care facility, or whatever? Does the home supply the special services or programs the physician considers necessary?

Is the home approved for participation in the Medicare or Medicaid programs? If you will depend on financing through one of these programs, then obviously this is an important question. But even if you plan to pay your own bills, the fact that a home meets Federal as well as State standards should be a point in its favor.

Does the home have an opening? If not, what is the likely waiting period? Many homes have waiting lists. Some put people on the list according to the date they apply. Others consider the elderly person's condition and the family's need to place the person in a home, and assign a position on the list accordingly.

What are the home's admission qualifications? Nursing homes vary widely in this respect. Some require that pa-

NURSING HOMES

tients be able to care for themselves to a certain extent. Some admit only patients who have been residents of the State. Some require proof or assurance in writing that you will be able to pay the bills. Some will not accept patients with serious mental disorders. Be wary of any nursing home representatives who insists that the patient sign over his personal and real property in exchange for care.

Getting recommendations. In addition to telephoning the nursing homes, try to find as many people as you can who are familiar with the homes on your list. Ask them which homes they do and do not recommend.

VISITING NURSING HOMES. By telephoning homes and getting people's opinions, you should be able to narrow the list. Now plan to visit each of them.

It is important to go to the homes in person *before* you make your choice. Only by seeing them firsthand can you get a true impression of the places and the people who work there. And only in this way will you be able to rest assured that you have made the best possible choice.

Because a nursing home is a complex operation, there are many things to find out when you visit. The following pages provide a general guide, with the emphasis on things to *do*. The checklist in the back of this booklet gives more specific points to look for and ask about. Take the booklet along and refer to the checklist during your visits.

Preparing for visits. For the first visit to a home, it is a good idea to make an appointment in advance. State that you would like to meet with the administrator—also, if possible, with the director of nursing services and the director of social services. Mention that you would like to watch a meal being prepared and served, and to see as many different therapy sessions and patient activities as possible.

Usually, a good time to visit is late morning or midday. By then the early morning cleanup is over and you will be in time for the noon meal.

A short time before your visit, review this booklet to refresh yourself on important points.

MEETING WITH KEY PERSONNEL. When you arrive at a home, spend some time with the administrator, the director of nursing services, and the director of social services. Talk with them long

NURSING HOMES

enough to get a feeling for the kind of people they are and their attitudes toward their work. Do not worry about imposing on their time, meeting with you and others like you is part of their job.

Encourage the people in the meeting to tell you about the history and philosophy of the home. Find out who owns the home and whether it is run on a profit or non-profit basis. (Under Federal regulations, the names of a home's owners and board members must be made available to the public.)

Verifying vital points. This is the time to check the state licenses or letter of approval from the licensing agency for the facility and for the administrator. Ask to see them, and look for dates to make sure the licenses are still in effect.

This is also the time to confirm that the home is certified for participation in the Medicare and Medicaid programs, and can provide any special programs or therapy the elderly person needs.

Checking reports of surveys. Reports from the State survey agency can give important clues to the health and safety conditions in the home: the Skilled Nursing Facility Survey Report, the Intermediate Care Facility Survey Report, and the Fire Safety Survey Report.

Each nursing home that participates in Medicare (as a skilled nursing facility) or in Medicaid (as a skilled nursing facility or an intermediate care facility) must be surveyed by the State at least once every 12 months to determine if it meets Federal standards. A review of these reports will show any deficiencies the facility may have.

Each report and accompanying statement of deficiencies and written comments are available to the public within 90 days following completion of the survey.

- *Medicare* survey reports are available at any local Social Security Office.
- The statements of deficiencies and written comments are available at the Social Security District Office, and public assistance agency servicing the area in which the nursing home surveyed is located.
- The State Welfare Department is responsible for establishing procedures for the disclosure of survey information for facilities participating only in the *Medicaid* program. Contact your local public assistance agency for information on the location of survey reports for skilled nursing facilities participating in Medicaid only and for reports on intermediate care facilities.

NURSING HOMES

Keep in mind, however, that no nursing home can participate in Medicare and/or Medicaid if it has serious deficiencies which place the health and safety of the patients in jeopardy. In addition, deficiencies noted on the report form must be corrected by the facility within a reasonable length of time.

Reviewing the statement of patients' rights. Ask for a copy of this statement; the home is required to make it available to the public. Note whether it covers the points required by Federal regulations as described in Part Two. During your visit, look for signs that patients' rights are actually being honored. You should also ask to see a copy of any Admission Agreement or Contract that the home may use.

CHECKING WITH THE STATE NURSING HOME OMBUDSMAN. Each State is now required by law to have a State Nursing Home Ombudsman. An important role of the ombudsman is to investigate and resolve complaints made by or on behalf of residents in nursing homes. The ombudsman is particularly concerned with any problems that may adversely affect the health, safety, welfare, and rights of nursing home residents. You may wish to check with the ombudsman to find out whether there are any serious complaints from residents in the nursing home you are considering. A listing of the State Nursing Home Ombudsman offices is in the Appendix of this publication.

TOURING THE HOME. You should be given a tour of the home by the administrator (if possible) or some other member of the staff. Look around carefully as you go, and feel free to ask questions about anything you do not understand.

General Observations. Try to see all the important areas of the home. Here are some things to look for in all areas of the nursing home:

Note the general appearance and atmosphere of the home. It should be pleasant, comfortable, attractively furnished and decorated. There should be touches that make it seem more like a home. Though the home may have a "lived-in" look, it should definitely be clean.

The home should also be reasonably free of unpleasant odors. This is a matter that requires some judgment. Where patients lack control of the bowels and bladder, *some* odors are to be expected, particularly in the early morning.

Prevention of accidents must be a major concern in nursing homes. Objects should not be left where patients may bump into

NURSING HOMES

them or trip over them. There should not be conditions that could lead to slips, such as wet spots or loose rugs on floors. In addition, nursing homes should always have devices to help patients steady themselves, such as handrails in hallways and grab bars in bathrooms and toilets.

Residents' rooms. For most residents, no part of the home is more important than their own rooms.

Visit some of the residents' rooms; they should be clean, comfortable, and pleasant. Ask about the procedures the nursing home takes to ensure that roommates are compatible.

Try to get an idea of how many beds in the home are occupied. In most areas, the good nursing homes are almost always occupied to near-capacity.

Each bedroom should have no more than four beds, a window, and access to the corridor. Mirrors in the room should be arranged for convenient use by residents in wheelchairs as well as by patients in a standing position. In rooms with more than one person, there should be fire resistant screens or curtains to ensure privacy.

In addition, each resident should have:
- an adjustable bed with a comfortable mattress and pillow
- adequate closet space (wardrobe, locker, or closet) with a clothes rod and adjustable shelf provided
- a bedside cabinet or table
- a comfortable non-folding chair
- a reading lamp
- a readily available individual bedpan, urinal, and/or washbasin and access to a lavatory or toilet room.

Each home should have enough over-bed or over-chair side tables to meet the needs of the residents. At each bed and in each toilet, bathing, and shower room, there should be within easy reach an automatic call button connected to the nearest nurses' station.

Ask how the home selects roommates. Putting two people together without considering their special interests, cultural background, and personalities can lead to conflict.

MEDICAL AND NURSING SERVICES. Because medical and nursing care are crucial to resident's welfare, you will want to find out as much about them as you can.

NURSING HOMES

If the elderly person will depend on the nursing home's physician, make a point of meeting him either at the home or later, in his office. Find out how often he visits and whether he actually sees residents, and how often he reviews their records. Ask what arrangements have been made for handling emergencies in the home and for making emergency transfers to a hospital. (You also might check with the hospital to find out their emergency procedures.)

Visit the nurses' station (the headquarters for the nursing staff). Ask for an explanation of the nurses' calling system by which residents can signal for help.

Ask to be shown the room where drugs are stored and prepared. Find out how drugs are safeguarded and who is authorized to administer them.

RESTRAINTS. On occasion, there may be a need for physical and/or chemical restraints. Restraints must be prescribed by the doctor, and should be used only when required to protect the health and safety of the patient. When a chemical restraint (medication) is used, a nurse must check the patient periodically to make sure there are no adverse side-effects. When a physical restraint is used, the patient should be monitored even more often to see that all is well, and to take care of any physical needs such as toileting. Ask about the nursing home's procedures with regard to checking on patients when restraints are used, and try to observe how the other patients seem to be faring.

Rehabilitation and activities programs. The efforts made to help residents regain their physical capacities and to provide them with satisfying recreational activities also deserve special attention.

Ask to see the schedule of events for the week. Note how often therapy sessions are scheduled and whether a variety of recreational activities is offered.

Try to see physical therapy, occupational therapy, and speech therapy in action. If this is not possible, at least visit the areas where these programs are conducted. If the therapists are on hand, make a point of talking with them. Ask to look at craft projects that residents in occupational therapy have completed or that are in progress. Watch a recreational activity in progress.

Food services. Obviously, the health and morale of residents is very much affected by the quality of the food they get. This is another area where you can rely heavily on your own experience.

NURSING HOMES

Inspect the kitchen. Although it is geared to serve a large number of people, it should be just as clean and orderly as your own kitchen at home.

Watch the kitchen staff in action for a while. They should function as a well-organized team. Look for signs that foods needing refrigeration, such as milk, cream sauces and mayonnaise, are not left standing on counter tops.

Ask to see the menus for the week. Are the meals interesting and varied? Is a snack offered at bedtime? Are between-meal snacks available during the day? Are the meal times at usually accepted hours of the day?

Ask about how special diets are handled. You should see special menus for therapeutic diets—low salt, low fat, and so on—and there should be some system for identifying patients who require these special meals.

Notice the food being prepared or served. It should be appetizing and attractive. Check whether it corresponds to the posted menu and adequate substitute food provided.

Ask to sample the food. (In some nursing homes, you may be invited to eat a meal in the dining room.) Is the food tasty? Would you be happy eating food of that quality day after day?

Watch patients eating a meal and note whether the patients appear to be enjoying the food. Are people who need it given help with eating, both in the dining room and in their own rooms? Are those who do not care for the food given something else they like better that has the same nutritional value?

MAKING FOLLOW-UP OBSERVATIONS. Consider going back for a second visit, particularly if you are unsure about anything. If you come during visiting hours, the administrator should not object. The best time to plan a second visit is during the evening hours, when there are usually fewer staff members on duty.

Take a leisurely walk through the facility, and try to determine answers to the following questions:

- Do the residents seem to receive attention in the evening?
- Are staff attitudes the same in the evening as during the day?
- Are there any evening activities for the residents?
- Does the evening staffing seem to be adequate to meet resident needs?

NURSING HOMES

Take time to chat with residents about how they feel about care in the nursing home. Their attitudes may be very revealing.

CHECKING COSTS AND OTHER ARRANGEMENTS. If all or part of the resident's bill will not be covered by the Federal insurance plans or other benefits, you will naturally be concerned about costs. Even Medicare and Medicaid do not cover all of the costs of care for residents in a nursing home.

Costs may vary from one nursing home to another. If you look carefully, you should be able to find a home that provides quality care at a reasonable price.

Charges. Unfortunately, billings are sometimes complicated, and different homes handle them in different ways. This may make it difficult to estimate what a typical month's bill will be and to compare the cost of one home with another.

Nearly all nursing homes have a basic monthly charge. Most also make other charges as well. The difficulty comes because there is no uniformity in determining which things are covered under the basic charge and which are "extras."

Usually the basic charge covers *at least* room and meals, housekeeping, linen, general nursing care, medical records services, recreation and personal care and similar services and materials that are provided equally to all patients. Generally, extra charges are made for items that vary from patient to patient.

These are extras in most nursing homes:
- Physician services, including the work of specialists like dentists, ophthalmologists, podiatrists, etc.
- Drugs and medications
- Physical therapy
- Diagnostic services such as laboratory work, x-rays, electrocardiograms, etc.
- Personal services such as telephone calls, personal laundry, beauticians and barbers.

Additional items are considered by many homes as part of the basic charge, whereas in other homes they are considered as extras. Included in this category are such items as the administration of drugs, examinations, special diets, and help with daily activities such as eating and bathing.

NURSING HOMES

Medicare will pay for items and services furnished by a SNF that are necessary for the care of the patient. Medicaid will also pay for the care and services needed by the patient. However, some items such as drugs may not be fully covered by Medicaid in some States. Under Medicare, after 20 days, there is a co-insurance amount that must be paid by the patient.

Private pay residents may be billed once for the length of a patient's stay, as a flat charge each month, or each time a service or material is provided. For example, a nursing home may make a one-time-only charge for a special mattress, may rent a wheelchair by the month, and may make a charge each time a person is given an injection or fed by hand.

Some other important matters. Here are some other financial and legal questions that should be answered.

> Will a refund be made for unused days paid in advance? It is common practice to pay the monthly charge in advance, but a person may not stay in the home for the full month. Some homes keep the full payment anyway, others make a refund for the unused days.
>
> If a resident's cash or other assets are entrusted to the home, determine how these are handled and accounted for. The resident should be given a signed receipt for all deposits, all withdrawals should be noted on a monthly or quarterly statement of funds, prepared and signed by the nursing home administrator. In this way, the patient can keep track of his or her account.
>
> Before a final choice is made, be sure you have a clear understanding about the following matters:
>
> - The daily rate, and exactly what is and what is not included in this rate.
> - The exact charges for supplies and services not included in this daily rate.
> - What will happen when personal funds are depleted and Medicaid (Title XIX) assistance is required.
> - What will happen if there is a change in the level of care needed by the patient.
> - The arrangements the facility has for pharmacy service.

NURSING HOMES

MAKING THE DECISION. Once you have visited several nursing homes and have figured out about how much they will cost, you are ready to see how they stack up against one another. In making comparisons, you will find it helpful to fill out the checklist in this booklet for each of the homes. You may find that none of the homes you are considering meets all the points described in this booklet. But keep in mind that some of the questions are more important than others, so simply adding up the "yes" and "no" answers will not give you a fool-proof basis for comparison. You must also use your own judgment. And if you are not sure how important an item is to the particular person who needs the home, a telephone call to his or her physician should help you decide.

If at all possible, do not let costs be the only factor you consider in choosing a home. The *quality* of care is critical. And by all means, let the elderly person play a part in making the decision.

MAKING THE SELECTION. For most people, finding ways to finance nursing home care is a major concern. If the elderly person does not qualify for care under Medicare or Medicaid programs, check whether his or her private health insurance covers nursing home costs. Retirement and pension plans may also include such coverage.

The contract. The nursing home may refer to this by one of several names: financial agreement, admission agreement, entrance contract, or some other term. What it amounts to is a contract between the nursing home and the patient spelling out the conditions under which the patient is accepted. The resident, or the person sponsoring him or her, will have to sign the contract before the patient is admitted and will be legally bound by what it says.

The contract should state the costs, the services included, legal responsibilities, and any other matters of a legally binding nature. Ideally, it should also include safeguards for the patient—patients' rights, grievance procedures, minimum nursing care, emergency procedures, and standards of food service.

Before you sign the contract, be sure you understand it completely. Ask the nursing home adminstrator to explain anything that is not clear. If possible, have a lawyer review the contract before you sign it.

NURSING HOMES

Preparing for the patient's admission. The administrator and director of social services will make arrangements with you for admitting the elderly person to the home. If the person is to be transferred from a hospital, the physician and the hospital's social worker will also be involved in the planning.

Naturally, you should do everything you can to help prepare the elderly person for entering the home. The social services director can advise you on this and may take an active part by visiting the person in advance.

To ease the transition, try to be with the elderly person on admission day and stay a few hours to help him or her get settled in.

FOLLOW UP. Once the elderly person has entered the nursing home, your responsibilities continue. Try to visit the home as often as you can. Seeing friends and relatives can be a tremendous boost to the resident's morale.

WHAT TO DO WHEN YOU HAVE A COMPLAINT. No matter how good any nursing home may be, the time may arise when you question the care, services or environment of the home. Usually, the first step in resolving such a problem is to speak directly to the nursing home administrator or to the director of nursing or of social services. If the matter is not satisfactorily settled using this approach, your next step would be to bring the problem to the attention of the Nursing Home Ombudsman in your State. Write or telephone the Nursing Home Ombudsman to discuss the grievance. The address and telephone number of the State ombudsmen are listed in the Appendix.

NURSING HOMES

PART FOUR

Checklist

The following is a checklist of important points to consider in selecting a nursing home. You should find the checklist helpful in several ways: for brushing up on things to look for and ask about before you visit a home, for referring to as you talk with staff members and tour a home, and for sizing up a home after a visit and comparing it with other homes you have visited.

There are many items on the list, because nursing homes are complex operations. To cover all the items, you may have to make additional visits or follow-up telephone calls.

Some of the items will be difficult to find out on your own, so you will probably have to ask personnel of the home.

This checklist is offered to serve as a reference guide:

The name of nursing **Home A** is _____
The name of nursing **Home B** is _____
The name of nursing **Home C** is _____

	HOME A Yes/No	HOME B Yes/No	HOME C Yes/No
Is the home certified to participate in the Medicare and Medicaid programs?	☐ ☐	☐ ☐	☐ ☐
Does the nursing home have the required current license from the State or letter of approval from a licensing agency?	☐ ☐	☐ ☐	☐ ☐
Does the administrator have a current license?	☐ ☐	☐ ☐	☐ ☐
If the person you are placing requires special services, such as rehabilitation therapy or a therapeutic diet, does the home provide them?	☐ ☐	☐ ☐	☐ ☐

NURSING HOMES

	HOME A	HOME B	HOME C
	Yes/No	Yes/No	Yes/No
Is the general atmosphere of the nursing home warm, pleasant, and cheerful?	☐ ☐	☐ ☐	☐ ☐
Is the administrator courteous and helpful?	☐ ☐	☐ ☐	☐ ☐
Are staff members cheerful, courteous, and enthusiastic?	☐ ☐	☐ ☐	☐ ☐
Do staff members show patients genuine interest and affection?	☐ ☐	☐ ☐	☐ ☐
Do residents look well cared for and generally content?	☐ ☐	☐ ☐	☐ ☐
Are residents allowed to wear their own clothes, decorate their rooms, and keep a few prized possessions on hand?	☐ ☐	☐ ☐	☐ ☐
Is there a place for private visits with family and friends?	☐ ☐	☐ ☐	☐ ☐
Is there a written statement of patient's rights? As far as you can tell, are these points being carried out?	☐ ☐	☐ ☐	☐ ☐
Do residents, other visitors, and volunteers speak favorably about the home?	☐ ☐	☐ ☐	☐ ☐

LOCATION

	HOME A	HOME B	HOME C
Is the home near family and friends?	☐ ☐	☐ ☐	☐ ☐

GENERAL PHYSICAL CONSIDERATIONS

	HOME A	HOME B	HOME C
	Yes/No	Yes/No	Yes/No
Is the nursing home clean and orderly?	☐ ☐	☐ ☐	☐ ☐

NURSING HOMES

	HOME A	HOME B	HOME C
	Yes/No	Yes/No	Yes/No
Is the home reasonably free of unpleasant odors?	☐ ☐	☐ ☐	☐ ☐
Are toilet and bathing facilities easy for handicapped patients to use?	☐ ☐	☐ ☐	☐ ☐
Is the home well-lighted?	☐ ☐	☐ ☐	☐ ☐
Are rooms well-ventilated and kept at a comfortable temperature?	☐ ☐	☐ ☐	☐ ☐

SAFETY	HOME A	HOME B	HOME C
	Yes/No	Yes/No	Yes/No
Are wheelchair ramps provided where necessary?	☐ ☐	☐ ☐	☐ ☐
Is the nursing home free of obvious hazards, such as obstacles to patients, hazards underfoot, unsteady chairs?	☐ ☐	☐ ☐	☐ ☐
Are there grab bars in toilet and bathing facilities and handrails on both sides of hallways?	☐ ☐	☐ ☐	☐ ☐
Do bathtubs and showers have non-slip surfaces?	☐ ☐	☐ ☐	☐ ☐
Are there smoke detectors, an automatic sprinkler system, and automatic emergency lighting?	☐ ☐	☐ ☐	☐ ☐
Are there portable fire extinguishers?	☐ ☐	☐ ☐	☐ ☐
Are exits clearly marked and exit signs illuminated?	☐ ☐	☐ ☐	☐ ☐
Are exit doors unobstructed and unlocked from inside?	☐ ☐	☐ ☐	☐ ☐

NURSING HOMES

	HOME A Yes/No	HOME B Yes/No	HOME C Yes/No
Are certain areas posted with no-smoking signs? Do staff, residents, and visitors observe them?	☐ ☐	☐ ☐	☐ ☐
Is an emergency evacuation plan posted in prominent locations?	☐ ☐	☐ ☐	☐ ☐

MEDICAL, DENTAL, AND OTHER SERVICES

	HOME A Yes/No	HOME B Yes/No	HOME C Yes/No
Does the home have an arrangement with an outside dental service to provide patients with dental care when necessary?	☐ ☐	☐ ☐	☐ ☐
In case of medical emergencies, is a physician available at all times, either on staff or on call?	☐ ☐	☐ ☐	☐ ☐
Does the home have arrangements with a nearby hospital for quick transfer of nursing home patients in an emergency?	☐ ☐	☐ ☐	☐ ☐
Is emergency transportation readily available?	☐ ☐	☐ ☐	☐ ☐

PHARMACEUTICAL SERVICES

	HOME A Yes/No	HOME B Yes/No	HOME C Yes/No
Are pharmaceutical services supervised by a qualified pharmacist?	☐ ☐	☐ ☐	☐ ☐
Is a room set aside for storing and preparing drugs?	☐ ☐	☐ ☐	☐ ☐
Does a qualified pharmacist maintain and monitor a record of each patient's drug therapy?	☐ ☐	☐ ☐	☐ ☐

NURSING HOMES

NURSING SERVICES	HOME A Yes/No	HOME B Yes/No	HOME C Yes/No
Is at least one registered nurse (RN) or licensed pratical nurse (LPN) on duty day and night?	☐ ☐	☐ ☐	☐ ☐
Is an RN on duty during the day, seven days a week? (For skilled nursing homes)	☐ ☐	☐ ☐	☐ ☐
Does an RN serve as director of nursing services? (For skilled nursing homes)	☐ ☐	☐ ☐	☐ ☐
Are nurse or emergency call buttons located at each patient's bed and in toilet and bathing facilities?	☐ ☐	☐ ☐	☐ ☐

FOOD SERVICES	HOME A Yes/No	HOME B Yes/No	HOME C Yes/No
Is the kitchen clean and reasonably tidy? Is food needing refrigeration not left standing out on counters? Is waste properly disposed of?	☐ ☐	☐ ☐	☐ ☐
Ask to see the meal schedule. Are at least three meals served each day? Are meals served at normal hours, with plenty of time for leisurely eating?	☐ ☐	☐ ☐	☐ ☐
Are nutritious between-meal and bedtime snacks available?	☐ ☐	☐ ☐	☐ ☐
Are patients given enough food? Does the food look appetizing?	☐ ☐	☐ ☐	☐ ☐
Sample a meal. Is the food tasty and served at the proper temperature?	☐ ☐	☐ ☐	☐ ☐
Does the meal being served match the posted menu?	☐ ☐	☐ ☐	☐ ☐

NURSING HOMES

	HOME A	HOME B	HOME C
	Yes/No	Yes/No	Yes/No
Are special meals prepared for patients on therapeutic diets?	☐ ☐	☐ ☐	☐ ☐
Is the dining room attractive and comfortable?	☐ ☐	☐ ☐	☐ ☐
Do patients who need it get help in eating, whether in the dining room or in their own rooms?	☐ ☐	☐ ☐	☐ ☐

REHABILITATION THERAPY

	HOME A	HOME B	HOME C
	Yes/No	Yes/No	Yes/No
Is a full-time program of physical therapy available for patients who need it?	☐ ☐	☐ ☐	☐ ☐
Are occupational therapy and speech therapy available for patients who need them?	☐ ☐	☐ ☐	☐ ☐

SOCIAL SERVICES & PATIENT ACTIVITIES

	HOME A	HOME B	HOME C
	Yes/No	Yes/No	Yes/No
Are there social services available to aid patients and their families?	☐ ☐	☐ ☐	☐ ☐
Does the nursing home have a varied program of recreational, cultural, and intellectual activities for patients?	☐ ☐	☐ ☐	☐ ☐
Is there an activities coordinator on the staff?	☐ ☐	☐ ☐	☐ ☐
Is suitable space available for patient activities? Are tools and supplies provided?	☐ ☐	☐ ☐	☐ ☐
Are activities offered for patients who are relatively inactive or confined to their rooms?	☐ ☐	☐ ☐	☐ ☐

NURSING HOMES

	HOME A	HOME B	HOME C
	Yes/No	Yes/No	Yes/No
Look at the activities schedule. Are activities provided each day? Are some activities scheduled in the evenings?	☐ ☐	☐ ☐	☐ ☐
Do patients have an opportunity to attend religious services and talk with clergymen both in and outside the home?	☐ ☐	☐ ☐	☐ ☐

PATIENTS' ROOMS

	HOME A	HOME B	HOME C
	Yes/No	Yes/No	Yes/No
Does each room open onto a hallway?	☐ ☐	☐ ☐	☐ ☐
Does each room have a window to the outside?	☐ ☐	☐ ☐	☐ ☐
Does each patient have a reading light, a comfortable chair, and a closet and drawers for personal belongings?	☐ ☐	☐ ☐	☐ ☐
Is there fresh drinking water within reach?	☐ ☐	☐ ☐	☐ ☐
Is there a curtain or screen available to provide privacy for each bed whenever necessary?	☐ ☐	☐ ☐	☐ ☐
Do bathing and toilet facilities have adequate privacy?	☐ ☐	☐ ☐	☐ ☐

OTHER AREAS OF THE NURSING HOME

	HOME A	HOME B	HOME C
	Yes/No	Yes/No	Yes/No
Is there a lounge where patients can chat, read, play games, watch television, or just relax away from their rooms?	☐ ☐	☐ ☐	☐ ☐
Is a public telephone available for patients' use?	☐ ☐	☐ ☐	☐ ☐

NURSING HOMES

	HOME A	HOME B	HOME C
	Yes/No	Yes/No	Yes/No
Does the nursing home have an outdoor area where patients can get fresh air and sunshine?	☐ ☐	☐ ☐	☐ ☐

FINANCIAL AND RELATED MATTERS

	HOME A	HOME B	HOME C
	Yes/No	Yes/No	Yes/No
Do the estimated monthly costs (including extra charges) compare favorably with the cost of other homes?	☐ ☐	☐ ☐	☐ ☐
Is a refund made for unused days paid for in advance?	☐ ☐	☐ ☐	☐ ☐
Are visiting hours convenient for patients and visitors?	☐ ☐	☐ ☐	☐ ☐
Are these and other important matters specified in the contract? (See page 29)	☐ ☐	☐ ☐	☐ ☐

BASIC FUNDAMENTALS OF GERIATRIC NURSING
CONTENTS

	Page
SECTION I. INTRODUCTION	1
1. General	1
2. Qualities Needed by the Specialist in Geriatric Nursing	1
3. Physiological Changes in the Geriatric Patient	2
4. Reaction of Nursing Personnel to Geriatric Patient	3
5. Additional Time Required by the Patient	3
II. GENERAL NURSING CARE MEASURES	4
6. Bathing and Skin Care	4
7. Sleep and Rest	4
8. Clothing	5
9. Exercise and Recreation	5
10. Elimination	5
11. Enemas	6
12. Nutrition	6
13. Communication	6
14. Diseases of Old Age	6
15. Needs of Geriatric Patient	7
16. Special Precautions	9
17. Role of the Health Nurse in Geriatric Care	9

BASIC FUNDAMENTALS OF GERIATRIC NURSING

Section I. INTRODUCTION

1. General

a. *Definition of the Aged Person.* Chronological age does not make anyone young or old. Some people are young in spirit at age 90; others are old at 21. However, the chronological age of 65 is arbitrarily considered the dividing point between the middle-aged and the aged or old person. This is the age when retirement from active employment generally takes place and when Old Age and Survivors Insurance (Social Security) benefits commence.

b. *Geriatric Nursing.* Geriatric nursing can be defined as caring for persons aged 65 or older. It cuts across many other fields of nursing, incorporating basic principles of nursing care. The specialist caring for a geriatric patient will utilize principles found in medical-surgical nursing, gynecological nursing, and psychiatric nursing, to mention only a few. Geriatric nursing in many ways is like any other type of nursing, yet in other ways it is different or special. What makes geriatric nursing special or different and how the specialist should act and react when caring for the elderly patient is the purpose of this chapter. Largely, the change lies in the approach, attitude, and personal warmth of nursing personnel, plus a knowledge of the aging process.

c. *Importance of Geriatric Nursing.* The ability to provide adequate and safe nursing services to the older age group is becoming of paramount importance. Between **2000,** and **2030** the percentage of the U.S. population over 65 years of age is expected to quintuple. More and more, elderly persons are found both within the civilian and the military hospital environment; this is expected to continue and even expand. It is a well-known fact that people are living longer. Medical science has made giant strides in the maintenance of health and the prevention of disease, as well as in curing disease and rehabilitating persons following disease or injury.

2. Qualities Needed by the Specialist in Geriatric Nursing

a. A specialist who assists with a geriatric patient will need to be emotionally stable and slow to anger, a condition known as maturity. The aged may be talkative, secretive, hostile, rude, and childish, but the specialist must not take their remarks personally. He must try to understand their behavior and react in a nonjudgmental manner.

b. The specialist must express sincere interest and affection for the geriatric patient. Old people recognize and detest insincerity. All nursing personnel should be kind, tolerant, and patient, but geriatric nursing personnel *must* be. These qualities come only when you have gained true respect for yourself; respect will then be given to others.

c. The specialist must also have empathy (a projection of one's own personality into the problems and personality of another; a feeling *with* someone). If a specialist can imagine that he has lost his job, lost his friends, lost his sensory perceptions, lost his home, lost his ability to speak fluently, lost his health, and lost his self-esteem, then he can begin to understand the disagreeable stubborn outbursts of an old person. He must recognize that hostility may be an expression of fear, and stubbornness may be an expression of insecurity. He must also recognize the embarrassment that would follow the failure to do even a simple task for oneself.

d. The specialist cannot become emotionally involved with the patient. Life can be prolonged, but death always awaits the geriatric patient. It requires a special quality to show affection for these old people and yet maintain a realistic acceptance that death will surely come.

e. The specialist must make observations for the nurse and doctor, as he will be with the patient more than they will.

3. Physiological Changes in the Geriatric Patient

The process of aging begins at birth and stops only with death. It is a very gradual process, yet the changes occur in a fairly predictable pattern, with the rate of change varying from one individual to another. It is a period that is often marked by mental confusion and vagueness. The specialist must consider this confusion and help the patient as much as possible. He must also be aware that the old person's body has undergone many other changes. The physiological changes that are seen in the geriatric patient can be generally classified as loss of elasticity in tissues and a general slowing down of

Table 1. Physiological Changes

System	Changes	Results in
Skeletal	Degenerative changes in joints. Decalcifieation-"mineral starvation" or demineralization	Pain and stiffness in joint. Fractures.
Muscular	Less muscular activity.	Slumped posture; sagging abdominal muscles; contractures.
Skin-Integumentary	Becomes dry; wrinkled, less elastic. Less oils produced. Baldness. Increased pigmentation.	Traumatized easily. Susceptible to deeubitus ulcers.
Circulatory	Degeneration of elastic tissues in blood vessels; thinning of middle layer of arterial wall; deposition of metabolic substances such as calcium and cholesterol on inner layer of arterial wall.	Impaired circulation; slower healing.
Respiratory	Rib cage rigid and less elastic; atrophy of respiratory muscles; lungs smaller; bronchioles less elastic; alveoli larger and less elastic with inner walls; vital capacity reduced.	Lowered efficiency of respiratory system.
Digestive	Less muscle tone; less mobility; less absorption of food; mucous membrane thinner; loss of tone in supportive structures.	Elimination problem; malnutrition; intestinal tissue traumatized.
Urinary	Efficiency of glomeruli reduced; muscular portion of ureter, bladder, and urethra less elastic; loss of tone of supportive structure; less blood supply.	Tissues easier traumatized and subject to infection. Reduced efficiency of urinary system.

the physiologic process. Table 1 illustrates some of the major changes.

4. Reaction of Nursing Personnel to Geriatric Patient

a. Some nursing service personnel may express displeasure when assigned to give care to aged people, often making such comments as "I'd much rather take care of an active duty soldier than that old retired sergeant," or "I just don't know how to handle old people." But retired sergeants or old people in general are not a group unto themselves; they are merely people who have grown old as everyone must do. As with any other person, however, they have certain basic needs, and these needs must be met if the optimum benefit from hospitalization is to be realized. Everyone needs recognition, security, and love. The nursing care plan should recognize these needs and try to satisfy them as nursing care is given.

Table . 2 Rules for Care of the Aged

DO-	DO NOT-
Treat as an individual.	Do not call old people "grandma" or "grandpa."
Call by name such as Sergeant Brown or Mrs. Green.	Do not stick to the procedure just for the procedure sake.
Be tolerant, patient, and kind.	Do not shout.
Speak slowly and distinctly.	Do not do *everything* for the patient.
Help the patient to help himself.	Do not ignore so-called minor complaints.
Be extremely observant.	Do not try to change lifelong habits of eating or sleeping.
Be optimistic.	

b. As the medical specialist cares for an aged patient, he must remember that the patient is a product of his heredity and long years of environmental pressures. The so-called, well-adjusted older person was probably a well-adjusted adult and child; whereas the so-called poorly adjusted older person who is garrulous at times and seemingly unreasonable was probably a poorly adjusted adult and child. It must be emphasized here that the habits of a lifetime will not be changed lightly or willingly; therefore, changes should be required only when absolutely necessary. *For example,* if an old person is used to having coffee at 5 o'clock every morning, he should be given the coffee at the hospital. Any adjustments that must be made should be made by the specialist, not the patient.

5. Additional Time Required by the Patient

a. The admission of an aged person on a busy ward can be disruptive. Routines geared to the adult or younger patient just do not meet the needs of the geriatrics patient. Adjustment of the routine and personnel is not without difficulty, but if the medical specialist is to fulfill his responsibility of providing nursing care, it must be done. Older patients cannot and should not be rushed, particularly in the morning. An older patient will take almost twice the time, for example, to prepare for breakfast as the younger patient. As medical specialists, you must be aware of the time involved and plan accordingly.

b. Many times it will seem easier and quicker to do something for the patient, rather than let him do it for himself, because it takes him so long. However, oversolicitous care and too much waiting on a patient will force him into a dependent role, a role he does not want and one that is incompatible with a healthy outlook on life. Avoid the temptation to take over. The aim of nursing care is to permit the patient to do as much for himself as he can, with only a minimum of assistance from nursing personnel. His small accomplishments will mean a lot to him.

Section II. GENERAL NURSING CARE MEASURES

6. Bathing and Skin Care

a. Older people do not need to bathe or be bathed daily. In fact, some medical geriatric specialists believe that once or twice weekly is sufficient. As a person ages, the skin dries because less oil is produced. Too frequent bathing might lead to skin irritation. However, areas that are soiled are bathed as needed.

b. If at all possible, the patient should be placed in a tub.

CAUTION

An elderly patient is always assisted to get in and out of a tub.

A tub bath provides an excellent opportunity to exercise all of his joints, as well as make him feel more comfortable. If getting in a tub is not possible, a wooden chair or stool should be placed in the shower or stall and the spray shower used. During the bath, whether in the tub or shower, the patient should be afforded privacy. A call light or bell should be in easy reach, and you should check on him frequently. If you cannot leave a patient because of safety reasons, do not look at him directly, but give the appearance of looking somewhere else in order to spare him embarrassment. If a patient becomes ill during a tub bath, pull the plug in the tub first and look after him. Do not leave him alone; wait for help.

c. If a patient is confined to bed, a bed bath once or twice a week, supplemented by partial bed baths and frequent massage to pressure points (but *not* to extremities) is sufficient. Since aged skin is easily traumatized, massage must be gentle. Use of alcohol should be avoided since it will tend to dry already dry skin. Use of a lanolin-rich lotion, particularly to the pressure point such as heels, elbows, and buttocks, will help. Extremities are not usually massaged because of the danger of disturbing blood clots.

d. Toenails and fingernails need careful attention. When possible, the geritric patient should be encouraged to do his own fingernails. Care of the toenails will probably have to be done by the specialist. Cutting nails or clipping cuticles too short must be avoided. If the toenails are long and horny, the physician should be informed since the services of a podiatrist may be indicated.

CAUTION

Never cut the toenails of a *diabetic* patient without a doctor's order. A break in the skin on the toe of a diabetic patient could lead to an amputation.

e. As a part of the daily routine, men should be encouraged and assisted, if necessary, to shave and to comb their hair. Use of an aromatic aftershave lotion can do much to raise the morale, especially if someone comments on it. Women, likewise, should be encouraged to fix their hair and put on makeup if they usually use it. If patients are unable to do for themselves, then the specialist should attend to these matters.

7. Sleep and Rest

a. The aged person needs warm sleeping garments and warm lightweight covers. A bed with adjustable height should be used, whenever available. If only a standard hospital bed is available, a footstool should be provided for the patient. He should be as comfortable as possible since he does not sleep as soundly as the younger patient. He will often wander up and down the ward corridors in the middle of the night. Because of this, there should be sufficient night personnel on duty and sufficient light for the patient's safety. Sonu patients will need side rails. A night snack, a glass of warm milk, or early morning coffee will help keep them more contented. Since old people sleep less at night, they tend to take naps during the day. A comfortable chair for them to doze in may rest them more than getting in and out of bed. (In fact, the exertion required for them to get into bed may wake them up.) A tap bell should always be placed near the chair when a patient is sitting up, so that he may use it if needed.

b. More rest is needed by the geriatric patient, yet too much rest can be dangerous, if not fatal. If the doctor permits, get the patient out of bed into a chair or a wheel chair at least daily. This not only aids him physiologically, but also improves his emotional outlook by providing a change of environment.

8. Clothing

Part of any admission routine is usually to have the patient remove his own clothing and wear hospital attire. In some situations, it is necessary and desirable to wear hospital pajamas, but to the older patient, loss of his clothing may mean another step down the road of dependence. Sometimes hospital routines must be bent some to allow, *for example,* the patient to wear his "long John's" as pajamas, if that is what he is accustomed to wearing-provided, of course, that he changes them and that either he or his family can care for them. Most older patients will dislike robes; they seem too much like sleeping garments to them. Women will like cotton smocks and men some type of shirt and loose slacks. They will often insist on long underwear-and they are right to do so. It is warmer and prevents skin surfaces from touching which, in turn, prevents chafing and soreness. At all times, clothing for old people should be soft, warm, and easily put on or cared for. Their morale will also be helped by color and style.

9. Exercise and Recreation

a. Exercise. Motion and exercise are important aids to circulation of blood and of lymph. It also aids elimination. Inexperienced personnel may be afraid that exercise may hurt the patient; the opposite is true. The aged patient is rarely ever put on complete bedrest. A comfortable rocking chair may be sufficient exercise; however, the doctor will order the most beneficial exercise possible. The nursing care plan should include instructions about exercise or ambulation.

b. Recreation. Old people need to be kept busy. Younger patients, if treated on the ward, can be utilized to interest the older patient in doing some activity, even if it is only talking to the geriatric patient. If possible, a dayroom or a separate room should be set aside for recreational activities. Since old people tire easily and often have limited powers of concentration, these activities must be limited to things that do not confuse or tire them. Games, religious services, and entertainment should be short. Then other factors enter

- Cost is important. Old people are generally on limited budgets.
- Projects should have a goal-not just be "busy" -perhaps a display, a sale, contest, newspaper coverage, or art show.
- Projects must be simple and individual enough so that each patient can do something. Remember some will be confused, some can work only under directions, some have trembling hands.
- Projects must be safe.

Some suggestions for recreation are group singing (use old familiar songs generally), drawing or painting pictures, dancing, knitting or sewing by hand (even men may enjoy this), quilting, checkers, dominoes, and puzzles.

10. Elimination

a. Bowel movements are one of the primary concerns of the elderly. Evacuation *does* become a problem with advancing age. Muscle tone decreases; there is less ability to chew and therefore less bulk in the diet; and exercise is limited. Regularity is important. The specialist can check to find out when the patient usually has a bowel movement. The patient may be accustomed to sitting on a commode for long periods of time. If at all possible, try to maintain his routine and schedule. The specialist should watch closely for signs of impaction such as dribbling diarrhea and notify the nurse if this occurs. In addition, elderly patients need bulk in their diet (whole grain cereals, leafy vegetables, fruit pulps and skins; these must be cooked thoroughly or chopped if patient has chewing difficulties). Often 5 or 6 prunes in the morning are sufficient to cause a bowel movement, but individual tolerances differ greatly. Some have found their own solution; let them use it, unless contraindicated. Medication for bulk may also be ordered by the doctor. Follow directives for giving this medicine carefully.

WARNING

Be sure to answer signal lights promptly. Older people often cannot wait, especially to urinate. Older male patients may feel more secure if allowed to keep a urinal in the bed or on a chair nearby.

b. Prostate trouble is common among old men. Early symptoms which appear very gradually are frequency, difficulty in initiating the flow, and difficulty in maintaining the flow. Hematuria and the symptoms of cystitis may also occur. Many malignancies occur here, so be sure to report incipient trouble.

11. Enemas

Older people need enemas more often than younger people but, if used too often, they will interfere with normal bowel movements and wash out the mucus that lubricates the colon. Enemas are given as for other adults but a bedpan or commode should be at hand as old people cannot always control their bowel movements.

12. Nutrition

Eating should be an enjoyable experience. Pleasant conversation, a neat area, and adequate time are essentials for this enjoyment. The food that can be eaten depends on the condition of the teeth. Baby food with added seasonings is used in some cases. Proteins are essential. Also, old people are as apt as children to swallow pieces of bone or gristle and choke. They should be given small servings on an attractive tray, with perhaps a flower, a special name card, and a colorful napkin. If their food must be cut up, do so before serving them to avoid chilling the food and also to avoid embarrassment to the patient. (He may even refuse to feed himself because of his shaking hand. If this happens, try giving him only one food at a time.) Soups and liquids are easier to handle in a lightweight cup from which he can drink. He will probably need help to open such things as milk cartons and individual packets. Whether or not he feeds himself, note what he eats and how much. The specialist should offer fluid at frequent intervals to the elderly patient since the patient may not be able to help himself. Make sure if the patient has dentures that they are in his mouth at meal time. The patient may be too forgetful or too confused to ask for them.

13. Communication

a. The older patient may have to be hospitalized at a time when his speaking and hearing ability are beginning to fail. He needs to communicate badly but may not be aware of his difficulty. He may accuse you of mumbling. He may and often does misunderstand the doctor. You will have to explain to him repeatedly as he will also forget what he is told. He may learn to cover up for his failure to hear by nodding, smiling, and pretending. This is quite common. You might ask him to tell you what you said. Above all, be patient.

b. Deafness can be suspected when there is a loss of interest in group activity, in what you say, and in other people; when he attempts to lip read or seems to hear better when he can see your face; and when he apparently ignores orders or suggestions.

c. Remember that communication may be difficult with the aged person even when he can hear-probably 50 years lie between you. You even have different standards; in your world of casual exposure, you may not realize that exposed knees can embarrass an old woman. You think of hospitals as a place where you go to get well; to the old, hospitals are places where you go to die. Be sure that you are really communicating what you want him to know or do.

14. Diseases of Old Age

Some of the diseases of old age are shown in table 3.

15. Needs of Geriatric Patient

The geriatric patient needs all of the following:
- Friends and family
- Maximum self-determination
- Privacy
- Individual expression
- Personal dignity
- New experiences
- Comfort and safety

Most of all, he needs to feel needed.

Table 3. Some Diseases and Conditions of Old Age

Disease or condition	What it does and what specialist may notice	Suggestions to specialist
Arteriosclerosis (hardening of the arteries).	Interferes with sight, speech, and circulation of the aged. Causes forgetfulness, particularly of recent events; changes in personality.	Be sure to repeat instructions many times in a slow, calm, deliberate manner. Patient who "runs away" may have just gone for a walk and forgot where to go. Be patient, and do not scold.
Eyes-Cataracts	Results in dimming of vision, progressing into blindness. Has difficulty in reading small print.	Have a stronger light for reading. Give large print for reading matter. Report any complaint referable to eyes to the nurse such as spots before eyes, burning sensation, tearing. If patient has surgery, be alert for unusual reaction to sedative. If eyes are bandaged, always announce your presence.
Ears-deafness	Makes communication difficult and may cause the patient to withdraw.	Speak slowly and deliberately.
Osteoarthritis	Causes pain on motion and swelling of the joints. Patient is afraid to move.	TCL is essential but do not encourage self-pity. Change position frequently, if bedfast. Encourage movement of all joints.
Fractures	Causes immobility of patient. May mean loss of independence, invalidism, or death to the patient.	Encourage patient to do as much for self as possible. Ambulate as soon as doctor permits. Change position frequently. If casted, watch for development of pressure points. Report to nurse or doctor any swelling, cyanosis, or blanching of skin.
Skin-Loss of sensation	Causes patient to tolerate pressure that would cause younger persons to turn to relieve pressure. Skin may turn red.	Report any redness of skin to doctor or nurse. See that the patient turns frequently. Massage only on doctor's orders. It is dangerous to massage extremities, particularly if patient complains of pain, because it might result in an embolus.

-Pruritis	Results from loss of oil. Causes intense itching. Results in excoriation of skin.	Use lanolin-rich lotion; bathe less frequently.
Arteriosclerotic heart disease.	Causes multiple small clots, which interfere with circulation to the heart muscle. Symptoms of cardiac failure, such as shortness of breath, fatigue, dependent edema.	Use slow motions. Allow patient to rest the moment he feels tired. Patient may breathe or sleep better when head is elevated.
Peripheral vascular disease	Decreases circulation to extremities because the circulatory system breaks down. Patient may complain of cold feet, numbness, tingling, or loss of feeling.	Use loose fitting socks or booties in bed. Use patient's shoes or slippers with firm soles if out of bed. Keep feet clean; soak as a part of bath.
Cerebrovascular Accidents (CVA).	Results in strange behavior, dizzy spells, forgetfulness, and confusion. Aphasia (loss of speech) and paralysis may occur.	Encourage patient to do as much as possible for self. If aphasic, talk to patient, not about him; he may understand more than he shows. Have patient use pencil and paper as a means of communication if possible. Protect against injury; *for example,* support in wheel chair and use bed side rails.
Cancer	Can result in mutilating surgery. May be cured. Often seen as a terminal case. Because of this, the word can cause extreme fear and anxiety. Patient may be apathetic or extremely anxious.	Attend to patient's physical needs as promptly as possible. Keep as comfortable as possible through nursing measures: turn frequently, give back rubs, and give medication for pain when requested by patient. Listen to patient; you may be his "sounding board." Encourage family to visit frequently.
Diabetics	Causes poor circulation and slow healing of injuries. A small injury to foot may result in amputation.	Encourage him to eat all food on tray, report what is left to nurse. Old people may act like children when confronted with a diet. They may get candy bars or refuse to eat. Foot care is extremely important. Keep extremely clean; give immediate care to any broken area; cut nails and fingernails only on doctor's orders and then very carefully. Check shoes for proper fit; hose or socks must not have mends or ridges.

Disease or condition	What it does and what specialist may notice	Suggestions to specialist
Pneumonia	Often causes light cough, drowsiness, and apathy. Patient may not appear as ill as he is.	Keep patient comfortable, often in a low Fowler's position. Put a pillow against the lower back or elevate the head of the bed on shock blocks. May be more comfortable in a chair but avoid exerting him, as pneumonia places a strain on the heart.
Tuberculosis	Causes cough and sputum. Common among elderly people, especially men. May not look as sick as he really is.	Teach him how to protect others but make allowance for his habits. If he will not use tissues, get soft rags that can be burned. While patient is in the hospital, he should be referred to the Health Nurse for contact investigation and for patient and/or family education on tuberculosis. If he is returned home, the Health Nurse should continue involvement in the case, checking him and his family by periodic contact followup and public health supervision of patient and family in the home.

16. Special Precautions
- Be especially alert to any confusion following sedation. Old people often have adverse reactions to sedatives and to medications given for pain.
- If a heating pad or hot water bottle is ordered by the physician, check frequently for condition of skin. Older people have a tendency to poor circulation and decreased sensation in their extremities. The patient may not realize the heating pad is too hot until he is burned.
- If postural drainage is necessary, try merely elevating the foot of the bed first as this may be enough, or put the patient's head at the foot of bed, placing the side with the affected lung uppermost and raising the knee gatch. He must be watched closely as he may not be able to tolerate it. Unless specifically ordered, the elderly patient is never placed crosswise on the bed with his head resting on the floor.
- If oxygen is ordered, give the geriatric patient special assurance. He may think this is a last resort and that he is dying.
- Insure that aged patients get frequent periods of exercise alternating with frequent periods of rest.
- Insure that he has proper ventilation. This is essential, since the decreased chest expansion and impaired circulation decrease the oxygen supply to the tissues. Do not put a geriatric patient in a draft, however.

17. Role of the Health Nurse in Geriatric Care

Because the older patient's illness may be a long one, with alternating periods of hospitalization and home care; because he may be alone and need special guidance; because of the need for special instructions to his family, the Health Nurse is usually consulted in health problems involving geriatrics. The time of her involvement will be decided by the doctor or nuise, but it will probably be *before the patient returns home*. The specialist should furnish her with any information requested.

GLOSSARY OF GERIATRIC NURSING TERMS

Aide — A person who acts as an assistant.

Ambulatory — Term referring to the ability to move at will.

Analgesic — An agent that alleviates pain without causing loss of consciousness.

Anemia — Medical diagnosis of a condition in which the blood is deficient in red blood cells, in hemoglobin, or in total volume. Types of anemia include aplastic anemia, B-12 deficiency (pernicious) anemia, folic acid deficiency anemia, or sickle cell disease.

Antipyretic — An agent that reduces fever.

Aphasia — Defect or loss of the power of expression by speech.

Arteriosclerosis — A condition marked by loss of elasticity, thickening, and hardening of the arteries.

Baseline data — Data or information collected which is necessary to identify needs, develop programs and meet those needs, and to measure the overall success of the initiatives undertaken.

Bathing — Process of washing the body or body parts. It includes taking a sponge, shower, or tub bath and getting to or obtaining the bathing water or equipment.

Campaign Survey(s) — Surveys of long term care facilities conducted solely as a data collection process with no formal relation to the certification procedure under Title XVIII and XIX.

Cathartic — A medicine that quickens and increases the evacuation from the bowels.

Chronic — Marked by long duration or frequent recurrence.

Clinical status — Measure of the stage and severity of illness.

Comatose — Pertaining to a state of profound unconsciousness from which the patient cannot be aroused, even by powerful stimulation.

Communication	A system of significant symbols which permit ordered human interaction.
Consultant	Qualified individual who provides professional advice or services.
Continence	Physiologic process of elimination from the bladder and bowel, if required.
Demographic characteristics	Profile of personal characteristics, including age, sex, marital status, and race.
Dentition status	Description of the number, kind, and arrangement of teeth in the jaw.
Decubitus ulcer	Break in the skin exposing deeper tissue caused by pressure on soft tissues while patient is lying down. Two other names which refer to the same condition are bedsores and pressure sores.
Diabetes	A deficiency condition marked by habitual discharge of an excessive quantity of urine; particularly diabetes mellitus.
Diagnosis	Common basis for defining patient needs for care and in organizing patient care services.
Dietitian	A person who has a baccalaureate degree and has completed a dietetic internship or coordinated undergraduate program approved by the American Dietetic Association, or who has the equivalent of such education and training.
Digestive	Pertaining to the process or act of converting food into materials fit to be absorbed and assimilated.
Discharge summary	Information from the transferring facility concerning medical findings, diagnoses, functional status, and response to previous treatment and care, as well as orders to initiate care of the patient.
Drug administration	An act in which a single dose of an identified drug, or combination of drugs, is given to a patient.
Dysarthic	Term referring to the imperfect articulation in speech.
Edentulous	Condition which occurs when all teeth are missing; toothlessness. If a person has a set of plates and does not use them, he is classified as edentulous.

Endocrine	Pertaining to internal secretions; applied to organs whose function is to secrete into the blood or lymph a substance that has a specific effect on another organ or part.
Facility personnel	Persons employed by the nursing home.
Fire door	A fire-resistive door assembly, including frame and hardware, which under standard test conditions, meets the fire protective requirements for the location in which it is to be used.
Fire partition	Floor-to-ceiling partition capable of retarding or stopping fire at a tested, specified rate.
Flame retardant	Having or providing comparatively low flammability or flame-spread properties.
Fracture	A broken bone.
Functional status	Measure of the degree of ability to cope with the activities of daily living.
Geriatrics	A branch of medicine that deals with the problems and diseases of old age and aging people.
Governing body	An identifiable authority in every nursing home having full legal and moral responsibility for all aspects of facility operations. This authority might be called "governing body," "board of directors," "board of trustees," or other appropriate designation.
Health care facilities	Facilities defined in terms of State licensure requirements that are designed for individuals with health needs.
Hypertension	Medical diagnosis of a condition in which there exists an abnormally "high" blood pressure measurement.
Incontinence	Involuntary loss of urine and/or feces.
Indwelling catheter	A hollow cylinder passed through the urethra into the bladder and retained there to keep the bladder drained of urine.
Licensed practical nurse (LPN)	A nurse who is a graduate of an approved school of practical nursing and/or is licensed by waiver to practice as a practical nurse. Also named licensed vocational nurse (LVN).

Life Safety Code	Publication of the National Fire Protection Association, which includes those requirements which are intended to provide a reasonable degree of safety against fire.
Long term care	Services for symptomatic treatment, maintenance, and rehabilitative services for patients of all age groups in various health care settings.
Intermediate care facility (ICF)	Facility certified by the Federal Government to provide an intermediate level of care. Facility providing health related care and services to individuals who do not require the degree of care and treatment that a hospital or SNF is designed to provide but who do require care above the level of room and board.
Long Term Care Facility Improvement Campaign (LTCFIC).	An accelerated project directed toward upgrading the quality of care provided in the Nation's nursing homes.
Medicaid	Health care coverage under Title XIX of the 1965 amendments to the Social Security Act (Public Law 89-97).
Medical director	The physician designated to help ensure the adequacy and appropriateness of the medical care provided to patients/residents.
Medical record	Clinical documentation of an individual's medical care.
Medical record administrator	A registered record administrator who has successfully passed an appropriate examination conducted by the American Medical Record Association, or who has the equivalent of such education or training.
Medicare	Health care coverage under Title XVIII of the 1965 amendments of the Social Security Act (Public Law 89-97).
Medication	Any substance or drug that is taken orally, injected, inserted, or topically or otherwise administered to a patient.
Mental illness	A medical diagnosis of psychosis, anxiety, depression, or other psychiatric illness.
Neoplasm	Any new and abnormal growth such as a tumor.

Neurological disorders	Diseases of the central nervous system and peripheral nerves.
Nursing home(s)	Facilities which provide some level of nursing care, participating in the Medicare (Title XVIII and Medicaid (Title XIX) programs.
Nursing home administrator	Person who is fully responsible for the day-today operation of the nursing home.
Nursing service	Patient care services pertaining to the curative, restorative, and preventive aspects of nursing that are performed and/or supervised by a registered nurse pursuant to the medical care plan of the practitioner and the nursing care plan.
Nutritionist	A person who specializes in the science of nutrition.
Orientation pattern	Range or degree of awareness of an individual within his environment, as to location, identity and time of day, month or year.
Ostomy	Surgical procedure that establishes an external opening into such parts of the body as the ureter(s), colon, ileum, etc.
Pathophysiologic	Descriptive term which refers to a variety of conditions and problems commonly described as accidental or developmental disabilities, chronic illnesses, and diseases of the aging.
Patient asessment form	Form developed which contains questions to be answered which describe the individual patient at the time of the survey. Data are provided about the patient's status from several perspectives: his physical functioning, impairments, medical risk status, and social demographic status.
Patient care policies	Policies adopted by the governing body of the facilities concerning the rules and regulations for the care of patients.
Patient care plan	A written program of care for the patient that is based on the assessment of individual needs, identifies the role of each service in meeting these needs, and the supportive measures each service will use to complement each other to accomplish the overall goal of care.
Pharmacist	An apothecary or druggist.

Physical therapist	An individual who is licensed by the State and is a graduate of a program in physical therapy approved by the Council on Medical Education of the American Medical Association and the American Physical Therapy Association, or who has the equivalent of such education and training.
Primary diagnosis	Medical description(s) of the main reason(s) for admission to facility.
Proprietary homes	Privately owned nursing homes. This category does not include those homes which are under voluntary nonprofit, Government, and religious auspices.
Region	A large territorial area that is delimited by the Department of Health and Human Services on the basis of geographic, economic, cultural, or a combination of the three categories.
Registered nurse (RN)	A nurse who is usually a graduate of a program in an accredited school of nursing and who is licensed to practice as a registered nurse.
Rehabilitative patient care	Equivalent to restorative patient care.
Resident	An individual domiciled in the intermediate care facility for the purpose of receiving specialty care.
Respiratory	Pertaining to the act of function of breathing.
Restorative nursing service	That aspect of nursing care oriented toward restoring an individual to his former capabilities.
Skilled nursing facility (SNF)	Facility certified by the Federal Government to provide a skilled level of care. Facility or nursing home for patients who require skilled nursing and rehabilitation services on a daily basis to help them achieve their optimal level of functioning.
Social worker	An individual who is registered by the State, where applicable, has received at least the baccalaureate degree and has met the requirements of a two-year curriculum in a school of social work that is accredited by the Council on Social Work Education, or who has the equivalent of such education and training.
Stroke	A sudden cerebrovascular accident.

Tranquilzer — An agent which acts on the emotional state, quieting or calming the patient without affecting clarity or consciousness.

Transfer agreement — A written arrangement to provide for reciprocal transfer of patients/residents between health care facilities.

www.ingramcontent.com/pod-product-compliance
Lightning Source LLC
Chambersburg PA
CBHW080933020526
44116CB00033B/2401